iNTERCOM 2000

Anna Uhl Chamot

Isobel Rainey de Diaz

Joan Baker de Gonzalez

Richard Yorkey

Heinle & Heinle Publishers
A Division of Wadsworth, Inc.
Boston, Massachusetts 02116

Publisher: Stanley J. Galek
Editorial Director: Christopher Foley
Project Editor: Anita L. Raducanu
Content Editor: Margot Gramer
Assistant Editors: Erik Gundersen
                 Nancy A. Mann

Production Supervisor: Patricia Jalbert
Production Manager: Erek Smith
Designed and Produced by: Publishers' Graphics Inc.
Prepress Color and Integration:
FinalCopy Electronic Publishing Services
Cover: The Graphics Studio/Gerry Rosentswieg

Acknowledgments

The authors and publisher would like to acknowledge the contributions of the following individuals who reviewed the *Intercom 2000* program at various stages of development and who offered many helpful insights and suggestions:

• Mary J. Erickson and Galen Shaney, *English Language Institute, University of Texas, Pan American*
• Toni Sachs Hadi, *New York City Board of Education*
• Katy Cox, *Casa Thomas Jefferson, Brasília, Brazil*
• Ronald A. Reese, *Long Beach (CA) Unified School District*
• Ruthann Hilferty, *Paterson (NJ) Board of Education*

• Lúcia de Aragão, Sonia Godoy, and Rosa Erlichman, *União Cultural, São Paulo, Brazil*
• Peggy Kazkaz, *William Rainey Harper College*
• Roland G. Axelson, Diane Hazel, and Mary Wayne Pierce, *Hartford (CT) Public Schools*
• Keith A. Buchanan, *Fairfax County (VA) Public Schools*

Contents

COMMUNICATION	GRAMMAR	SKILLS

COMMUNICATION	GRAMMAR	SKILLS

COMMUNICATION	GRAMMAR	SKILLS

Intercom 2000

The People

Tom Logan

MARITAL STATUS: married; 3 children

OCCUPATION: travel agent (Wells Travel Agency)

PASTIMES: working in the yard, listening to music

Adela Logan

MARITAL STATUS: married; 3 children

OCCUPATION: student and homemaker

SCHOOL: Winfield Technical Institute

MAJOR: computer programming

PASTIMES: listening to music, going to the movies

Sam Logan

AGE: 20 years old

MARITAL STATUS: single

OCCUPATION: mechanic (Winfield Garage) and student

SCHOOL: Winfield Community College

MAJOR: engineering

SPORTS: running, swimming

Bob Logan

AGE: 17 years old

SCHOOL: Winfield High School

SPORTS: basketball, soccer, tennis

BEST FRIEND: Mike Young

Lisa Logan

AGE: 12 years old

SCHOOL: Winfield Elementary School

ABILITIES: sings well

SPORTS: ice skating

BEST FRIEND: Joyce Young

Elinor Young

MARITAL STATUS: married; 4 children

OCCUPATION: doctor (Winfield Hospital)

PASTIMES: playing tennis, going for long walks, going to museums

Howard Young

MARITAL STATUS: married; 4 children

OCCUPATION: engineer

PASTIMES: playing tennis, swimming

Liz Young

AGE: 21 years old

MARITAL STATUS: single

OCCUPATION: international telephone operator

LANGUAGES: German, French, Spanish

Mike Young

AGE: 17 years old

SCHOOL: Winfield High School

SPORTS: soccer, basketball, tennis

PASTIMES: dancing

BEST FRIEND: Bob Logan

Ted Young

AGE: 15 years old

SCHOOL: Winfield High School

SPORTS: soccer, swimming

Joyce Young

AGE: 12 years old

SCHOOL: Winfield Elementary School

ABILITIES: draws well

SPORTS: soccer, basketball

BEST FRIEND: Lisa Logan

Pablo Nava

MARITAL STATUS:
married; 2 children

OCCUPATION:
architect

ADDRESS:
Calle Paloma, 5
Mexico, D.F.,
Mexico

Melanie Nava

MARITAL STATUS:
married; 2 children

PLACE OF BIRTH: Los
Angeles, California

OCCUPATION: English
teacher

PASTIMES: travel,
photography

Carlos Nava

AGE: 18 years old

PLACE OF BIRTH:
Mexico, D.F.,
Mexico

OCCUPATION: student
(last year of high
school)

LANGUAGES: Spanish
and English

Ana Nava

AGE: 14 years old

PLACE OF BIRTH:
Mexico, D.F.,
Mexico

OCCUPATION: student

LANGUAGES: Spanish
and English

Maria Gomez de Nava

MARITAL STATUS:
widowed; 1 child
(Pablo Nava)

ADDRESS:
Calle Paloma, 5
Mexico, D.F.,
Mexico

Gino Leone

PLACE OF BIRTH: Naples, Italy

OCCUPATION: cook (Roma Restaurant) and cooking teacher (Winfield Community College)

SPORTS: swimming

GIRLFRIEND: Cristina Silva

Cristina Silva

PLACE OF BIRTH: Bogota, Colombia

OCCUPATION: cashier (Roma Restaurant) and student

SCHOOL: Winfield Community College

MAJOR: art history

PASTIMES: dancing

BOYFRIEND: Gino Leone

Gloria Rivera

AGE: 16 years old

SCHOOL: Winfield High School

PLACE OF BIRTH: New York City

SPORTS: volleyball

ABILITIES: plays the guitar well, sings

Toshio Ito

PLACE OF BIRTH: Kyoto, Japan

OCCUPATION: flight attendant (World Airlines)

LIKES: travel, working with people

SPORTS: swimming

Nhu Trinh

PLACE OF BIRTH: Saigon (currently Ho Chi Minh City), Vietnam

OCCUPATION: flight attendant (World Airlines)

PASTIMES: going to the movies

Sekila Manzikala

PLACE OF BIRTH: Kinshasa, Zaire

OCCUPATION: student

SCHOOL: Winfield Community College

ABILITIES: sings well

LANGUAGES: French, Lingala, English

UNIT 1

COMMUNICATION
Talking about past events ▪ Asking about past events ▪ Talking about movies ▪ Making suggestions ▪ Making plans

GRAMMAR
Simple past tense of regular and irregular verbs: affirmative and negative statements, Wh- and yes/no questions, short answers

SKILL
Reading a movie ad ▪ Writing a letter

What Did You Do Last Weekend?

Liz Young and Cristina Silva are on their way to work.

LIZ:	Hi, Cristina.
CRISTINA:	Hi, Liz.
LIZ:	Did you have a good weekend?
CRISTINA:	Yeah, it was OK.
LIZ:	What did you do?
CRISTINA:	Not much. On Saturday I stayed home and watched TV. On Sunday morning I visited some friends.
LIZ:	Sounds like you had a nice weekend. Ted and I went to see "What's So Funny?" Saturday night.
CRISTINA:	Oh, yeah? Did you like it?
LIZ:	No, I didn't like it at all. It was dumb!
CRISTINA:	Really? Did Ted enjoy it?
LIZ:	Yeah, he did. He likes comedies, but I like horror movies.
CRISTINA:	I like horror movies, too.
LIZ:	How about going to see "The Blob"? It's at the Winfield Theater this week. It's an old movie, but it's really good.
CRISTINA:	Great idea! How about Thursday night?
LIZ:	Sorry, I can't. I play soccer on Thursday nights. How about Friday night?
CRISTINA:	Friday? Yeah, I'm free on Friday. Let's meet at the Winfield.
LIZ:	Great! See you at the Winfield at 7:00 on Friday night!
CRISTINA:	OK. See you then, Liz!

1 Presentation

Talking about past events

> To form the simple past tense of regular verbs:
>
> visit ——→visit**ed**
> stay ——→stay**ed**
> BUT
> dance ——→dance**d**
> study ——→stud**ied**

A

On Friday night, Mike danced a lot.

B

On Saturday, he visited some friends.

C

On Sunday, he stayed home and studied.

2 Pronunciation

The past tense ending of regular verbs can be pronounced:
/t/; /d/; or /id/.

> On Saturday Lisa helped Tom.   /t/
> All of the Logans stayed home.   /d/
> On Sunday Lisa visited a friend. /id/

Read these sentences aloud.

1. Lisa called a friend.   /d/
2. Adela listened to music.   /d/
3. Bob wanted to stay home.   /id/
4. Mike washed the dishes.   /t/
5. Carlos passed his exam.   /t/

6. Ted looked for Liz.   /t/
7. Liz worked in a hospital.   /t/
8. They reported to the class.   /id/
9. Sam danced last night.   /t/
10. Adela studied a lot.   /d/

3 Practice

Complete the paragraph with the simple past tense of the following verbs:

call	talk	wash	study	help
cook	stay	listen	watch	clean

Last Saturday all of the Logans (1) _____ home, and they
were very busy. Bob (2) _____ a lot for his math exam.
Then he (3) _____ his room. Lisa (4) _____ TV
and (5) _____ Tom in the yard. Sam (6) _____
the car, and then he (7) _____ dinner. It was delicious.
After dinner Adela and Tom (8) _____ to music in the living
room. Lisa (9) _____ a friend, and they (10) _____
on the phone for a long time.

4 Presentation

Asking and telling about past events

Simple past tense: yes/no questions				Short answers		
Did	I you he she we they	stay home watch TV	Friday evening? last night?	Yes,	I you he	did.
				No,	she we they	didn't.

TED: Did you play basketball
yesterday, Bob?

BOB: Yes, I did. I played for
five hours.

TED: Did Sam play, too?

BOB: No, he didn't. He
stayed home.

5 Practice

Answer the questions. Give a short affirmative or negative answer and then give more information in an additional sentence.

> Did you study hard last night?
> Yes, _____I did_____ . _____I studied_____ for three hours.
>
> Did Gino visit Cristina last night?
> No, _____he didn't_____ . _____He visited_____ Sam.

1. Did Liz call a friend last night?
   Yes, _____ . _____ Nina.
2. Did the Youngs go shopping last Saturday?
   No, _____ . _____ home.
3. Did Lisa wash the dog on the weekend?
   No, _____ . _____ the car.
4. Did Ted play baseball last Saturday?
   No, _____ . _____ basketball.
5. Did Bob stay home last Friday?
   Yes, _____ . _____ math.
6. Did Tom and Adela watch TV on Saturday night?
   No, _____ . _____ to the radio.
7. Did Gino listen to music?
   No, _____ . _____ TV.
8. Did Adela relax on the weekend?
   No, _____ . _____ in the yard.
9. Did Mike dance a lot at the party?
   Yes, _____ . _____ for three hours.
10. Did Bob work hard on Saturday?
    Yes, _____ . _____ for eight hours.

6 Interaction

On a piece of paper write a list of eight activities, some of which you did and some of which you did not do last weekend. Exchange lists with a partner. Take turns finding out what each other did.

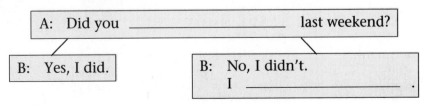

A: Did you _____ last weekend?

B: Yes, I did.

B: No, I didn't.
   I _____ .

7 **Presentation** 🔲

Asking and telling about past events

What			I	do?		I	went to a movie.
What (kind of) movie	did		you he she we they	see?		You He She We They	saw a comedy.
When				get home?			got home at 10:00.
Where				go?			went to Winfield.

A

LIZ: What did you do last Saturday night?
CRISTINA: I visited a friend.
LIZ: What did you do?
CRISTINA: We watched a movie on TV.
LIZ: What movie did you watch?
CRISTINA: "The Thing that Ate New York."

B

MIKE: What did Gloria do last Friday night?
SEKILA: She went to a party.
MIKE: What time did she get home?
SEKILA: At 10:00.

8 **Practice**

Work with a partner. Take turns asking and answering questions about the activities of the people in the chart below.

A: What did Mike do last Friday night?
B: He went to a party.
A: Was it a good party?
B: Yeah. He danced a lot.
A: What time did he get home?
B: At 1:00.

	Friday night	Saturday	Sunday morning	Sunday night
Mike	go to a party dance a lot get home at 1:00	visit a friend play basketball get home at 6:00	stay home wash the car	stay home cook dinner rice and meat
Bob	stay home study a lot math	work at the Roma get home at 11:30	go to the park play basketball get home at 12:30	stay home watch TV horror movie

9 Interaction

Make a chart like the one in *8*. Fill it out with information about your own
weekend. Then work with a partner and find out what each other did on each of
the days.

> A: What did you do last _____ ?
> B: I _____ . And what did you do?
> A: I _____ . And what did you do last _____ ?
> B: I _____ .

10 Vocabulary in Context

Movies

A

Ted likes **comedies** because they
are **funny.**

B

Joyce prefers **adventure movies**
because they are **exciting.**

C

Lisa likes comedies. She doesn't like
horror movies because they are
scary.

D

Gino likes **westerns** because they
are exciting and sometimes funny.
They usually tell a good story, too.

E

Elinor likes **dramas** because they
tell interesting stories. Sometimes
they are **romantic** and sometimes
they are **sad.**

11 Interaction

Work with a partner. Take turns asking and answering questions about movies. Here is a model.

A: Did you see a movie ___last Friday___ ?
B: Yes, I did.
A: What did you see?
B: ___"The Bear"___ .
A: What kind of movie is that?
B: It's ___an adventure movie___ .
A: Did you enjoy it?
B: ___Yes, I did___ . It was ___exciting___ .

12 Presentation

Talking about past events

Negative simple past tense statements

I You He She We They	didn't	go to school watch TV work hard dance at the party	yesterday. last night. last week.

1. Gino didn't watch TV last night. He went to bed early.
2. Joyce didn't go to school yesterday. She stayed home.

13 Practice

Today is Monday, November 12. Look at Joyce's diary from last week. Use the information there to correct the following false statements.

NOVEMBER	
MONDAY 5 *played soccer*	**FRIDAY** 9 *went to a party*
TUESDAY 6 *went to the library*	**SATURDAY** 10 *went to the movies with Lisa*
WEDNESDAY 7 *had pizza with Lisa*	
THURSDAY 8 *played soccer*	**SUNDAY** 11 *studied; played tennis with Ted*

Joyce played tennis last Thursday.

She didn't play tennis.
She played soccer.

1. Joyce went to the movies with Lisa last night.
2. Joyce watched TV last Friday.
3. Joyce studied last Saturday.
4. Joyce played tennis with Lisa yesterday.
5. Lisa had coffee with Joyce last Wednesday.
6. Joyce went to the pool last Tuesday.
7. Joyce played basketball last Monday.
8. Joyce went to school yesterday.

14 Listening

Number your paper from 1-5. Listen to the telephone conversation. Then read the following statements, and write *T* (True), *F* (False), or *M* (Maybe).

1. Adela had a great week.
2. Elinor worked hard last week.
3. Elinor liked the movie "A Cry in the Dark."
4. It was a comedy.
5. Adela would like to see a comedy this weekend.

Making suggestions; refusing and accepting

> **Why don't we** + verb?
>
> | **How** | **about** + noun? |
> | **What** |

ELINOR: **Why don't we** go to the movies tonight?
ADELA: Sorry, not tonight. I'm really tired.
ELINOR: **How about** Thursday night?
ADELA: Sorry, I can't. I go swimming on Thursdays. **What about** Friday night?
ELINOR: On Friday I have an art lesson. **What about** Saturday?
ADELA: Saturday's fine with me.
ELINOR: Good. See you at the theater at 7:00.

16 Practice

Work with a partner. Use the information in the chart to practice making suggestions, and accepting and refusing them.

Time	Student A	Student B
TONIGHT	free	music lesson
THURSDAY	free	work
FRIDAY	cook dinner	free
SATURDAY	free	free

A: Why don't we _____ tonight?
B: Sorry, I can't. I _____ tonight.
A: _____ Thursday?
B: I _____ on Thursdays. _____ Friday?
A: Sorry, I can't on Friday. I _____ .
B: _____ Saturday?
A: _____ fine. See you _____ .
B: Great! See you there.

17 Reading

Before You Read

1. Do you have friends or relatives who live far away?
2. Do you write letters to them?
3. What do you write to them about?

Ted's friend Tim is studying in London. Here is a letter that Ted wrote to him. However, the paragraphs in this letter are not in the correct order. Read the letter and reorder the paragraphs by numbering them 1-4.

10 South Kennedy Avenue
Winfield, New York 11500
USA
October 15, 1990

Dear Tim,

Do you go to the movies a lot in London? Joyce and I went to the movies last Friday. It was a comedy, and it was very funny. _____

I am playing a lot of soccer this month. I played for two hours yesterday. Then I went home and helped Mom. I cooked dinner, and it was delicious! I have to stop now. I'm going out with Mike tonight. Write soon. _____

I have a good friend in London. She's a student, too, and she knows London very well. Her name is Carol Hughes, and her address is 23 Pelham Street, London SW1. Her telephone number is 589-5100. Why don't you call her? Tell her you're my friend. She can introduce you to her friends. _____

Thank you for your letter. It was good to hear from you. I'm glad you like London, and I'm glad that the people are kind; but I'm sorry you don't have a lot of friends. _____

Yours, Ted

18 Writing

Write a letter from Mike to his friend Jim. Use the letter in *17* as a model and include the following information.

1. Jim is studying in Mexico.
2. Jim is living in Mexico City.
3. Mike has some nice friends in Mexico City.
4. They are the Nava family and their address is Calle Paloma, 5.
5. Mike went to the movies with Bob yesterday.
6. They saw a horror movie.
7. Mike didn't like the movie but Bob did.
8. Mike is playing a lot of tennis this month.
9. He played for three hours yesterday.
10. Then he went home and cooked lunch.

19 Final Activity

You meet a friend on the way to class. Follow the instructions for a conversation.

Situation:

STUDENT A: Last weekend you went to the movies. You liked the movie very much. It was a very romantic drama.

STUDENT B: Last weekend you went to the movies, too. You didn't like the movie. It was a very silly comedy.

A: Greet your friend.
B: Return greeting.
A: Ask about weekend activities.
B: Give details. Ask about his or her weekend activities.
A: Give details.
B: Suggest something to do for next Friday night.
A: Give a reason why Friday isn't possible.
   Suggest Saturday afternoon.
B: Agree to Saturday and suggest a time and place.
A: Agree to the time and place, and say good-bye.
B: Respond.

UNIT 2

COMMUNICATION
Asking for and giving directions ▪ Describing location ▪ Asking about location

GRAMMAR
There is ▪ There isn't ▪ Is there? ▪ Prepositions: *at the corner of, between, at the end of*

SKILLS
Reading a map ▪ Giving directions ▪ Reading a subway map

Is There a Bank Near Here?

Toshio is in front of the art museum on Main Street. He's asking a police officer for directions.

TOSHIO: Excuse me, Officer. Is there a bank near here?

OFFICER: Yes, there's a bank on Park Road. Go one block north on Main Street. Turn left at the corner of Main Street and Park. Walk a block and a half, and there's a bank on your left. Did you get that?

TOSHIO: I think so. Let's see . . . I walk one block north on Main Street to Park Road. I turn left and walk a block and a half. The bank is on my left.

OFFICER: That's right!

TOSHIO: Thank you, Officer. Just one more question. Are there any bookstores in Winfield?

OFFICER: Yes, there are two. There's a general bookstore and a college bookstore.

TOSHIO: Can you tell me how to get to them?

OFFICER: Sure. The general bookstore is just up this street on the left between the drugstore and the train station. Now, the college bookstore is pretty far. It's at the corner of Church Street and Ocean Avenue.

TOSHIO: At the corner of Church Street and Ocean Avenue? Oh, yes! I know that bookstore. Thanks for all your help, Officer.

OFFICER: You're welcome. Don't get lost!

1 Presentation

Describing location

Find the supermarket, City Hall, and the art museum on the map of Winfield. Then read the following conversation.

> TOSHIO: Where's the supermarket?
> SAM: The supermarket is **at the corner of** Main Street and Park Road.
> TOSHIO: And where's City Hall?
> SAM: City Hall is on Main Street **between** Warner's Department Store and the supermarket.
> TOSHIO: And the art museum?
> SAM: The art museum is **at the end of** Main Street.

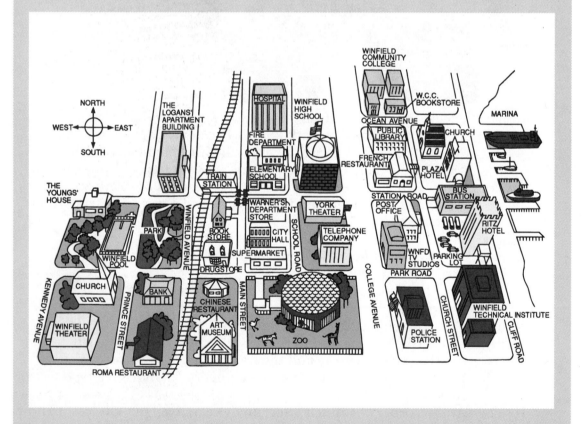

2 Practice

Use the map of Winfield to ask and answer questions about these buildings and places.

> the Roma restaurant / Prince Street
>
> A: Where's the Roma Restaurant?
> B: It's at the end of Prince Street.

1. the police station / College Avenue
2. the Youngs' house / Kennedy Avenue and Station Road
3. the fire department / School Road / the elementary school and the hospital
4. Warner's Department Store / Main Street and Station Road
5. Chinese restaurant / Park Road / Winfield Avenue and Main Street

3 Presentation

Talking about location with *there is (there's)*

> 1. There's a bookstore on Main Street.
> 2. There's a bus station on Church Street.
> 3. There's a traffic light at the corner of Main Street and Station Road.

4 Practice

Look at the map of Winfield and give one piece of information about the following streets.

> Kennedy Avenue
>
> There's a movie theater on Kennedy Avenue.

1. Winfield Avenue
2. Prince Street
3. Main Street
4. Church Street
5. Cliff Road
6. College Avenue
7. Ocean Avenue
8. School Road
9. Station Road
10. Park Road

5 Presentation

Asking about location with *there is*: questions and short affirmative answers

TOSHIO: **Is there** a park in Winfield?
SAM: Yes, **there is.**
TOSHIO: Where is it?
SAM: It's on Park Road.

6 Practice

Work with a partner. Use the map of Winfield on page 18 to ask for and give information about the following places.

a hospital
A: Is there a hospital in Winfield?
B: Yes, there is.
A: Where is it?
B: It's on Main Street.

1. a police station
2. a fire department
3. a train station
4. a high school
5. an elementary school

6. a community college
7. a supermarket
8. a zoo
9. a pool
10. a Chinese restaurant

7 Interaction

Working in pairs, think of ten important buildings or places in the town or city where you live; for example, *a zoo, an art museum*, etc. Then take turns being a tourist in the town or city. Ask for information about these buildings and places.

A: Is there _____ in _____ ?
B: Yes, there is.
A: Where is it?
B: It's on _____ .

8 Vocabulary in Context

Map directions

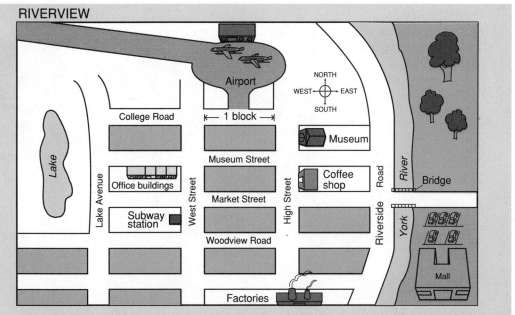

1. In Riverview, the river is **east of** the city, and the airport is **north of** the city.
2. Market Street is one block **south of** Museum Street, and High Street is one block **west of** Riverside Road.
3. Walk north on High Street. The coffee shop is **on your right.**
4. Walk west on Museum Street. The office buildings are **on your left.**

9 Practice

Answer these questions about Riverview. Use the map and the vocabulary from *8.*

> Where are the factories?
>
> They're south of the city.

1. Where's the lake?
2. Where's the airport?
3. Where's the mall?
4. Walk north on Riverside Road. Where is the bridge?
5. Walk north on West Street. Where is the subway station?
6. Walk east on Museum Street. Where are the office buildings?

10 Presentation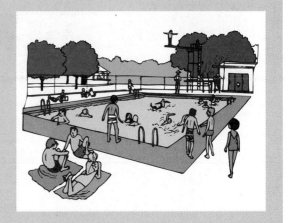

Asking about location with *there is*: short negative answers

A: Is there a lake in Winfield?
B: No, **there isn't**, but there's a pool.

11 Practice

Work with a partner and use the map of Winfield on page 18. Take turns asking and answering questions about the following buildings and places. Use the conversation model in *10*.

1. a mall
2. an Indian restaurant
3. a science museum
4. a lake

5. an airport
6. a Mexican restaurant
7. a Hilton Hotel
8. a subway station

12 Interaction

Ask and answer questions about the town or the part of the city you live in.

A: Is there | a | _____ in _____ ?
          | an |

B: Yes, there is.
    It's on _____ .

B: No, there isn't, but there's
    | a | _____ .
    | an |

13 Listening

Number your paper from 1-5. Listen to the phone conversation. Then complete each sentence with information from the conversation.

1. The caller is calling the _____ Museum.
2. He is going to the museum by _____ .
3. The bus stop for the museum is at the corner of
   (a) _____ and (b) _____ .
4. The museum opens at _____ .
5. The museum is open (a) _____ through (b) _____ .

14 Reentry

Describing a location

Look at the map of Winfield on page 18. Make sentences with one of these prepositions or prepositional phrases of location: *next to, near, across from, at the corner of, at the end of, between.*

> the drugstore
>
> The drugstore is at the corner of Park Road and Main Street.

1. the TV studio	4. the Roma	7. the supermarket
2. the Youngs' house	5. the bus station	8. City Hall
3. the pool	6. the art museum	9. the Plaza Hotel

15 Pronunciation

Pronounce these sentences.

1. Take the first street on your right.

2. Take the third street on your left.

3. Take the fourth street on your right.

4. Take the fifth street on your left.

16 Presentation

Asking for and giving directions

Look at the map of Winfield on page 18. Imagine you are at the elementary school and you want to go to the TV studio. You ask a police officer for directions.

> YOU: Can you tell me how to get to the TV studio?
> OFFICER: Sure. Go east on Station Road and take your first right. That's College Avenue. Walk one block. The TV studio is at the end of the block, at the corner of Park Road.

17 Practice

Work with a partner. Look at the map of Winfield on page 18. Take turns asking for and giving directions to a place in Winfield. Use the conversation model in *16*.

1. from the Roma to the Plaza Hotel
2. from the Plaza Hotel to the bank
3. from the zoo to the Roma
4. from the park to the art museum
5. from the hospital to the library
6. from the high school to the pool

18 Writing

Look at the map of Westlake. Write the directions for going from the fire department to another place in Westlake.

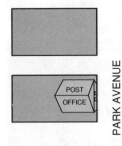

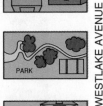

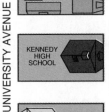
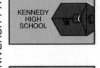
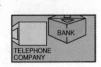

PARK AVENUE · WESTLAKE AVENUE · UNIVERSITY AVENUE · YORK AVENUE

MAIN STREET

FIRST STREET

FIRE DEPARTMENT · HOSPITAL · MODERN LANGUAGE INSTITUTE · UNIVERSITY THEATER · UNIVERSITY BOOKSTORE · UNIVERSITY · YORK HOTEL

POST OFFICE · PARK · DRUG STORE · WESTLAKE DEPARTMENT STORE · KENNEDY HIGH SCHOOL · BUS STATION

TELEPHONE COMPANY · BANK · SUPERMARKET · CHURCH

19 Interaction

Work with a partner. Use your paragraph from *18* to give him or her directions to a place in Westlake. Do not show your paragraph to your partner and do not tell him or her the destination. Your partner follows your directions using the map of Westlake. If he or she gets lost, try again.

20 Reading

Before You Read

1. Is there a subway system in your city or country?
2. Why do people use subways?
3. Why do some people prefer the bus?

> **Useful vocabulary**:
>
> 1. commuter rail = train for people going to work
> 2. ctr. = center
> 3. main = most important
> 4. change = go from one to another

Look at the map of the subway system in Boston, Massachusetts.

Comprehension

1. Name the two kinds of lines on this map: **a.** _____
   b. _____

2. Name the four subway lines:
   a. _____   **c.** _____
   b. _____   **d.** _____

3. Name the main stations where people can change subway lines:
   a. _____   **c.** _____
   b. _____   **d.** _____

21 Interaction

Use the map of the Boston subway system to ask for and give directions.

> A: Excuse me. How do I get from Broadway to State?
> B: Go north on the Red Line. Change at Downtown Crossing. Take the Orange Line and go north. State is the first stop.

1. from Boylston to Harvard
2. from Bowdoin to Central
3. from Harvard to Arlington
4. from Lechmere to Revere Beach
5. from Mattapan to Chinatown

22 Final Activity

Work with a partner. Draw a map showing your school and the area around it. Mark street names and places. For example, include: *stores, restaurants, parks, and libraries.*

STUDENT A: Start at your school. Give directions to a place on the map. Do not tell Student B what the place is. Can your partner follow your directions?

STUDENT B: Start at your school. Listen, follow Student A's directions, and find the place! Are you right?

Do this several times, changing roles.

COMMUNICATION
Describing the weather ▪
Asking for and giving temperatures ▪
Explaining past actions ▪ Talking
about the past

GRAMMAR
Simple present vs. present continuous ▪
Negative questions in the simple past tense ▪
Forming adjectives with nouns + -y

SKILLS
Understanding a weather report ▪ Reading a
weather map

The Weather's Terrible!

Sekila comes by to see Gloria. They talk about a party last night and about the weather.

GLORIA: Hi, Sekila! Come in! . . .
Why didn't you go to the party
last night?

SEKILA: Because it was so cold and rainy.

GLORIA: That's too bad! It was a really good
party. Hey, why don't we go for a
walk this afternoon, Sekila? I need
some exercise.

SEKILA: Go for a walk? But it's so cold out.

GLORIA: Cold out? What's the temperature?

SEKILA: About 50 degrees.

GLORIA: Fifty? That's not cold. Just wait until winter, Sekila.

SEKILA: Why?

GLORIA: Well . . . it snows a lot and sometimes it's *very* cold. Last winter it
was 10 degrees for three weeks. And it was windy, too.

SEKILA: That sounds awful!

GLORIA: It wasn't all that bad. The sun was out almost every day.

SEKILA: Look! It's raining again! This weather
is terrible!

GLORIA: Why don't we just sit down and have a
cup of coffee, then . . .
What's the weather like in Zaire, Sekila?

SEKILA: Well, every morning it's hot and sunny.
It rains every day, but just at noon and
only for an hour or two. Then the sun
comes out again.

GLORIA: Sounds great! When's the next flight
to Zaire?

1 Vocabulary in Context

Describing the weather

To describe the weather, use:
noun + -*y* = adjective

For example: cloud + -*y* = cloudy

What's the weather like?

A
It's cloudy.

B
It's rainy.

C
It's windy.

D
It's sunny.

2 Practice

Ask and answer questions about the weather.

40°F and .

A: What's the weather like?
B: It's cold and rainy.

1. 80°F and .

2. 20°F and .

3. and .

4. 70°F and .

5. 55°F and .

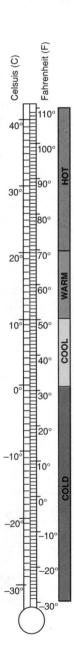

3 Practice

Work with a partner and write the names of five places in your country. Take turns asking and answering questions about the weather in these places in different months of the year.

> A: What's the weather like in Lima in January?
> B: It's warm and sunny.

4 Pronunciation

Pronounce these words.

1. Dallas
2. Denver
3. Boston
4. New York
5. San Juan
6. Detroit
7. El Paso
8. Miami
9. Seattle
10. Anchorage
11. Providence
12. Buffalo

5 Presentation

Contrasting: simple present versus present continuous

1. It rains a lot in Boston,

   and it's raining there now.

2. It snows a lot in Anchorage,

   and it's snowing there now.

> TED: Does it rain a lot in London, Tim?
> TIM: Yes, it does.
> TED: Is it raining there now?
> TIM: No, it isn't. It's snowing.

6 Practice

Practice talking about the weather in the following cities.

> rain / Dallas // no / but
> A: Does it rain a lot in Dallas?
> B: No, it doesn't, but it's raining there now.
>
> snow / Anchorage // yes / but
> A: Does it snow a lot in Anchorage?
> B: Yes, it does, but it isn't snowing there now.

1. rain / Bogota // yes / but
2. snow / Paris // no / but
3. rain / London // yes / but
4. rain / São Paulo // yes / and

5. rain / Mexico City // no / but
6. rain / Washington // yes / and
7. rain / San Juan // yes / but
8. snow / Buffalo // yes / and

7 Presentation

Asking for and giving temperatures

TED: What's the temperature in London today?
TIM: It's 1°C. That's about 34°F.
TED: And what was the temperature yesterday?
TIM: It was minus 2°C.
TED: Is that 28°F?
TIM: That's right.
TED: Wow! That's cold for November!

1°C = one degree Celsius
34°F = thirty-four degrees Fahrenheit

To convert Fahrenheit to Celsius: (a) subtract 32 (b) multiply by 5, and (c) divide by 9.
For example: (a)   51°F   (b) 19 x 5 = 95   (c) 95 ÷ 9 = about 10°C
　　　　　　　　　　 - 32
　　　　　　　　　　―――
　　　　　　　　　　 19

To convert Celsius to Fahrenheit: (a) multiply by 9, (b) divide by 5, and (c) add 32.

8 Practice

Take turns asking about and telling the temperatures in the following cities.

> Chicago / 55°F / 60°F
> A: What's the temperature in Chicago today?
> B: It's 55°F.
> A: That's . . . uh . . . 13°C, right?
> B: Yes, that's right.
> A: And what was the temperature yesterday?
> B: 60°F. That's 16°C.

		Today	**Yesterday**
1.	San Francisco	70°F	75°F
2.	Caracas	67°F	62°F
3.	London	59°F	57°F
4.	Montreal	34°F	30°F
5.	San Jose	88°F	90°F

9 Interaction

STUDENT A: Copy the first chart. Ask Student B for the information missing from your chart. Fill in the information.

STUDENT B: Copy the second chart. Ask Student A for the information missing from your chart. Fill in the information.

Student A		
Buffalo		
Caracas	warm and sunny	75°
Dallas	hot and sunny	80°
Denver		
Detroit	rainy and cool	50°
El Paso		
Lima		
Madrid	cloudy and warm	75°
Orlando	cool and rainy	60°
San Juan		
Tokyo	cloudy and cool	60°

Student B		
Buffalo	cold and snowy	30°
Caracas		
Dallas		
Denver	cool and cloudy	50°
Detroit		
El Paso	hot and sunny	90°
Lima	hot and cloudy	85°
Madrid		
Orlando		
San Juan	hot and sunny	95°
Tokyo		

> A: What was the weather like in _____ yesterday?
> B: It was ____° , and it was _____ and _____ .

10 Listening

Number your paper from 1-6. Listen to the weather report for New Hampshire and then complete the statements.

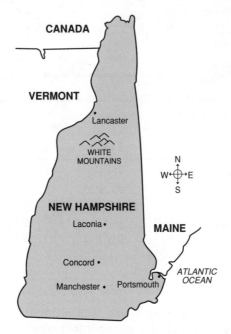

1. In the north it's _____ and _____ .

2. The temperature in Lancaster is ____ .

3. In the central part of the state, it's _____ .

4. The temperature in Laconia is ____ .

5. The southern part of the state is _____ .

6. The temperature in Concord is ____ .

11 Presentation

Talking about the past

> SEKILA: Did it rain a lot last winter?
> GLORIA: No, it didn't, but it snowed a lot.
> SEKILA: Oh, that sounds awful.

12 Practice

Ask and answer questions about the weather in the places in the chart.

City	January	February	March
London			
Chicago			
Moscow			
Atlanta			

A: Did it snow in London in January?
B: No, it didn't, but it rained a lot.

A: Did it rain in February, too?
B: Yes, it did. It rained a lot.

13 Presentation

Explaining past actions

GLORIA: Why didn't you go to the party last night?
SEKILA: Because it was so cold and rainy.

14 Practice

Work with a partner. Ask and answer questions about the following activities.

play tennis yesterday / cold
A: Why didn't you play tennis yesterday?
B: Because it was so cold.

1. go for a walk last night / cold and windy
2. play basketball last week / hot
3. go to the park yesterday / cold and rainy
4. drive to Chicago last month / rainy and windy
5. walk to school yesterday morning / cold

15 Reading

Before You Read

1. Does the weather change a lot where you live?
2. Do you listen to weather forecasts on TV or on the radio?
3. Do you read them in the newspaper?

Useful vocabulary:

1. thunderstorm (t'storm)
2. showers = rain, but not all the time
3. cool = not very cold

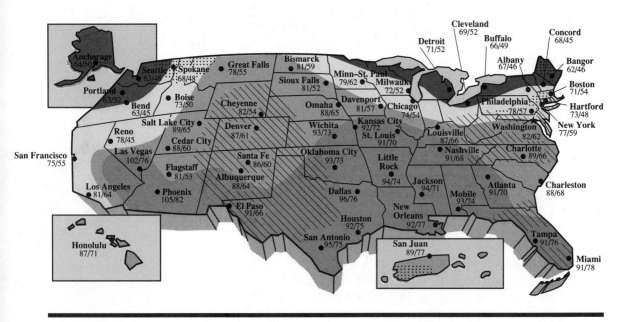

Legend Rain T'storms Showers Snow

Below 10 10s 20s 30s 40s 50s 60s 70s 80s 90s 100s

Temperatures on this page in Fahrenheit. Use scale to convert to Celsius.

Fahrenheit	0	10	20	30	40	50	60	70	80	90	100
Celsius	-18	-12	-7	-1	4	10	16	21	27	32	38

Anchorage 64/50
Seattle 63/48
Spokane 68/48
Great Falls 78/55
Bismarck 81/59
Minn–St. Paul 79/62
Milwaukee 72/52
Detroit 71/52
Cleveland 69/52
Buffalo 66/49
Concord 68/45
Albany 67/46
Bangor 62/46
Portland 63/52
Boise 73/50
Sioux Falls 81/52
Davenport 81/57
Chicago 74/54
Philadelphia 78/57
Boston 71/54
Bend 63/45
Cheyenne 82/54
Omaha 88/65
Hartford 73/48
New York 77/59
Salt Lake City 89/65
Denver 87/61
Wichita 93/73
Kansas City 92/72
St. Louis 91/70
Louisville 87/66
Washington 82/62
Reno 78/45
Cedar City 88/60
Nashville 91/68
Charlotte 89/66
San Francisco 75/55
Las Vegas 102/76
Santa Fe 86/60
Oklahoma City 93/73
Little Rock 94/74
Flagstaff 81/53
Albuquerque 88/64
Jackson 94/71
Atlanta 91/70
Charleston 88/68
Los Angeles 81/64
Phoenix 105/82
Dallas 96/76
Mobile 93/74
El Paso 91/66
Houston 92/75
New Orleans 92/77
San Antonio 95/75
Tampa 91/76
Honolulu 87/71
San Juan 89/77
Miami 91/78

Comprehension

A. Study yesterday's weather map for the United States and decide if the following statements are _True_ or _False_.

1. In Phoenix, it was very hot.
2. In Buffalo, it was cold.
3. In Reno, it was warm.
4. In Detroit, it was cool.
5. In Miami, it was very hot.
6. Boston had showers.
7. It snowed in Denver.
8. It rained in Chicago.
9. Washington had thunderstorms.
10. It was dry in San Juan, Puerto Rico.

B. Use the legend of the weather map to complete these statements.

1. 10°C is about _____ °F.
2. 80°F is about _____ °C.
3. _____°C is about 40°F.
4. _____°F is about 16°C.
5. _____°C is about 30°F.

16 Reentry

Describing geographical location

Look again at the weather map and describe the location of cities in the United States.

> Philadelphia / Washington
>
> Philadelphia is north of Washington.

1. Phoenix / Flagstaff
2. San Francisco / Los Angeles
3. Reno / San Francisco
4. Houston / Dallas
5. Atlanta / Charleston
6. Washington / Charlotte

17 Writing

Tim took a trip to Paris. He sent this postcard to Ted Young. Read the postcard.
Then imagine you are on vacation. Use Tim's postcard as a model and write a
postcard to a friend.

Dear Ted,
    I arrived here for a short vacation yesterday. This is a very beautiful city. Last night I went to the Latin Quarter and I had a delicious meal there. This morning the weather wasn't very good. It was rainy and windy, so I went to the Louvre. By the way, I called Carol. She's very nice.
    Say hello to everyone in Winfield.
                        Tim

Ted Young
10 South Kennedy Avenue
Winfield, New York
11500

*The Latin Quarter is the student section of Paris. The Louvre is an art museum.

18 Final Activity

Draw a map of your country or of the state you live in now. Mark three or four of
the major cities. Then draw weather symbols on the map to show how the
weather probably is today. Write temperatures on your map. Then, prepare a
short report to give to the class. Be sure to describe the location of the cities
(*north, south, east, west of*, or *in the . . . part of the state/country*.)

SYMBOLS:

sunny   rainy   windy

cloudy   snowy

REPORT: This is the state of Florida. Miami is in the southern part of the
state. In Miami it is sunny and warm. The temperature is 75°F.

UNIT 4

COMMUNICATION
Pointing out something far from you ▪
Talking about clothes ▪ Explaining
problems ▪ Identifying and asking for an
alternative ▪ Asking for information in a store

GRAMMAR
That and *those* ▪ *Too* + adjective ▪
The pronoun *one* ▪ *On the first, second,
third floor*

SKILLS
Reading a store ad ▪ Writing a note

Shopping for Clothes

Toshio Ito is at Warner's Department Store looking for a shirt.

SALESPERSON: Good afternoon, sir.
May I help you?

TOSHIO: Yes, thank you. I'd like
to see that shirt, please.

SALESPERSON: Which one, sir?

TOSHIO: The green one, next to
those blue socks.

SALESPERSON: Here you are.

TOSHIO: What size is it?

SALESPERSON: It's a medium.

TOSHIO: That's my size, but it
looks small. May I try it on?

SALESPERSON: Of course. The fitting rooms are over there on your right.

SALESPERSON: How does it fit?

TOSHIO: I think it's too tight. May I try a
large, please?

SALESPERSON: I'm sorry. I don't have a green one
in that size. How about this red one?

TOSHIO: OK, I'll try that. I like that color, too.
. . .

TOSHIO: Yes, this is perfect. I'll take it.
How much is it?

SALESPERSON: $30. Is that cash or charge, sir?

TOSHIO: Cash.

SALESPERSON: Anything else?

TOSHIO: No, thank you. Oh, yes, by the way,
are the coats on this floor?

SALESPERSON: No, they're on the fourth floor.

TOSHIO: Thank you.

1 Pronunciation

Pronounce these sentences.

> Which shirt, sir?
>
> The green one, next to those blue socks.

1. The yellow one, next to those white sneakers.
2. The gray one, next to those green shorts.
3. The beige one, next to those black suits.
4. The green one, next to those brown shoes.
5. The red one, next to those blue skirts.

2 Presentation

Pointing out things far from you

> Use **that** to point out something far from you.
> Use **those** to point out more than one thing far from you.

TOSHIO:	May I see **that** shirt, please?
SALESPERSON:	Which one, sir?
TOSHIO:	The green **one**, next to **those** blue socks.

One replaces a noun; in this case, **shirt**.

3 Practice

Work with a partner. Take turns asking to see the clothes.

A: May I see that dress, please?
B: Which one, | ma'am | ?
               | sir |
A: That yellow one, next to those white sneakers.

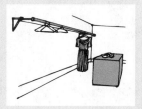

1.

4.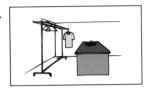

2.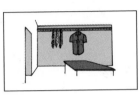

5.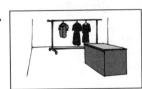

3.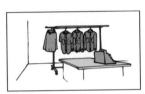

6.

4 Practice

Complete the following sentences with *that* or *those*.

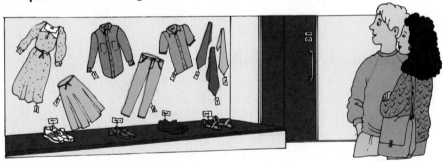

1. _____ sneakers are very expensive.
2. Yes, they are, and _____ dress next to the sneakers is very expensive, too.
3. I can't see the price of _____ shirt. It's probably not expensive.
4. Look at _____ shoes! The color is awful!
5. You're right, but _____ sandals are nice.
6. Yeah, and I like _____ blue skirt, too!
7. What do you think of _____ ties?
   The color's OK, but they're too wide.
8. I think _____ jeans are nice.
   Do you think they have my size?

5 Vocabulary in Context

Clothes

It's almost winter and the people in Winfield have to wear warm winter clothes. Everybody needs:

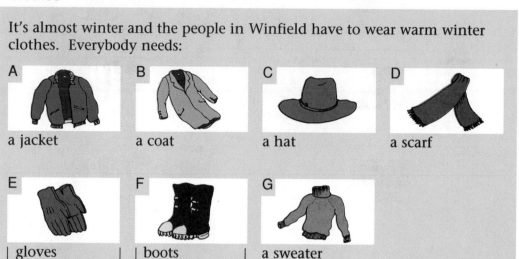

A	B	C	D
a jacket	a coat	a hat	a scarf

E	F	G
gloves a pair of gloves	boots a pair of boots	a sweater

6 Practice

Describe what these people are wearing.

This man is wearing a hat, a scarf, a coat, a pair of gloves, pants, and a pair of shoes.

1.

3.

5.

2.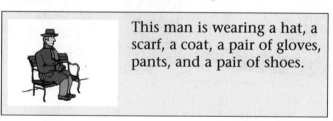

4.

6.

7 Reentry

Pointing out objects near you

Work with a partner. Ask and answer questions about the clothes.

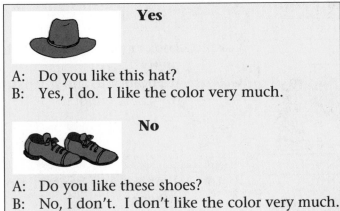

Yes

A: Do you like this hat?
B: Yes, I do. I like the color very much.

No

A: Do you like these shoes?
B: No, I don't. I don't like the color very much.

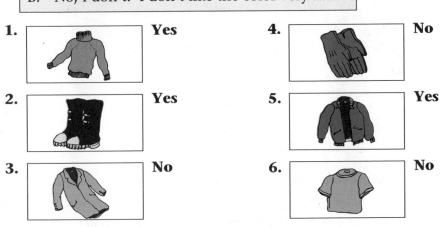

1. Yes
2. Yes
3. No

4. No
5. Yes
6. No

8 Practice

Look at the pictures and complete the conversations with *this, that, these,* or *those.*

A

TOM: Do you like (1) _____ scarf?
ADELA: It's nice, but (2) _____ scarves are nice, too, and they're only five dollars.

MIKE: What about Dad's birthday?
(3) _____ calculators are on sale.

LIZ: I think he'd like (4) _____ tie instead.

CRISTINA: Look at (5) _____ dress. Isn't it pretty?

GLORIA: It's beautiful, and it looks nice with (6) _____ shoes.

PABLO: I'm tired and hungry. How about lunch?

MELANIE: Well, (7) _____ Japanese restaurant has good food, and (8) _____ restaurant across the street is very good, too.

9 Presentation

Explaining problems with clothes

Use **too** + *adjective* to explain why you don't like or want something.

A

This dress is **too long.**

B

This shirt is **too tight.**

10 Practice

Explain the problem. Use words such as: *small, big, long, short, tight.*

This sweater is too small.

1.

2.

3.

4.

5.

6.

11 Presentation

Identifying an alternative

Use **a/an** + *adjective* + **one** to identify an alternative.

Adela is trying on a blue blouse, but she doesn't like the color.
She would like to try on **a green one** instead.

12 Practice

Say what these *Intercom 2000* characters are trying on and what they would like to try on.

> Gino / a black coat // gray
> Gino is trying on a black coat, but he doesn't like the color.
> He would like to try on a gray one instead.

1. Elinor / a white sweater // beige
2. Ted / a red scarf // blue
3. Lisa / a green skirt // brown
4. Tom / a yellow shirt // blue
5. Liz / a blue dress // purple
6. Howard / a red jacket // beige
7. Sam / a gray hat // brown
8. Gloria / a pink sweater // orange
9. Mike / a green shirt // black
10. Joyce / a black coat // brown

13 Presentation

Asking for an alternative in a store

> SALESPERSON: How does the blouse fit?
> CUSTOMER: Fine, but I don't like the color. May I see a blue one, please?
> SALESPERSON: I'm sorry. I don't have a blue one in your size.

14 Practice

Work with a partner. Take turns being the salesperson and the customer.

> shirt / ●
> A: How does the shirt fit, | sir | ?
> | ma'am |
> B: Fine, but I don't like the color. May I see a green one, please?
> A: I'm sorry. I don't have a green one in your size.

1. blouse / ○
2. shirt / ○
3. skirt / ●
4. suit / ●
5. dress / ○
6. coat / ●
7. jacket / ●
8. hat / ○
9. sweater / ○
10. T-shirt / ○

15 Listening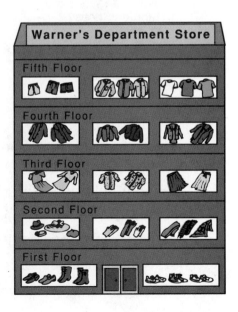

Adela is shopping for some clothes. Listen to the conversation. Then complete the following information.

1. Adela buys: Reasons:

    a. _____   _____

    b. _____   _____

2. Adela doesn't buy: Reasons:

    a. _____   _____

    b. _____   _____

16 Presentation

Asking for information in a store

The customer is on the third floor.

CUSTOMER:	Excuse me. Are the hats on this floor?
SALESPERSON:	No, they aren't. They're on the second floor, next to the gloves.
CUSTOMER:	Are the skirts on this floor?
SALESPERSON:	Yes, they are. They're over there.

17 Practice

Work with a partner. Take turns asking for information at Warner's Department Store. Use the conversation model in *16*. The number indicates the floor you are on.

1. 4 / shorts
2. 5 / coats
3. 1 / sneakers
4. 2 / dresses
5. 2 / scarves
6. 3 / blouses
7. 3 / boots
8. 4 / shirts
9. 4 / jackets
10. 1 / suits

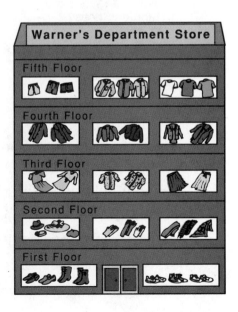

Warner's Department Store

Fifth Floor

Fourth Floor

Third Floor

Second Floor

First Floor

Before You Read

1. Do you buy things on sale?
2. Do you read the sale ads in newspapers?
3. What kind of information do you look for in sale ads?

Comprehension

Answer the following questions about the store ad.

1. How many different kinds of athletic shoes are there in this ad?
2. Can you buy women's tennis shoes on sale?
3. What's the regular price of the basketball shoes?
4. Which shoes are for men and for women?
5. Which shoes would you like?

19 Writing

Look at the note that Ted wrote to his sister, Liz. Then write a similar note to a member of your family about a pair of athletic shoes you bought.

Liz,
    When you go to Warner's could you please return my new basketball shoes. They're too small. Could you please get another pair in size 11? They're on sale and cost $67.99. The receipt is in the box with the shoes.
                              Thanks, Ted

20 Final Activity

In the United States, people sometimes return gifts to the store if they don't like them. Do people do this in your country?

Work with 4-5 classmates. Imagine that you each received an item of clothing for your birthday, but that you didn't like it. Copy the chart below. Fill in the chart by talking to your classmates about their gifts. Here is an example.

A: What did you get for your birthday, Sue?
B: I got a sweater, but I don't like the color. I would like a blue one instead.
A: Are you going to return it?
B: Yes, I am.

Name	Clothing	Problem	Return it?
Sue	sweater	color	yes

COMMUNICATION
Asking about materials ▪ Giving detailed
descriptions ▪ Talking about purchases ▪
Asking for and giving information about
where things are made ▪ Talking about
imports and exports ▪ Talking about a
country's products

GRAMMAR
Made of ▪ *Made in* ▪ Nouns used as
adjectives ▪ Past tense of *buy* ▪ More
uses of the simple present tense

SKILLS
Taking notes ▪ Reading a guidebook ▪
Writing a descriptive paragraph

Made in the U.S.A.

*This morning Sam and Toshio went to the art museum. Then they had lunch at
the Chinese restaurant. This evening they're at Gloria's house. They're telling her
about their afternoon activities.*

GLORIA: And what did you do this afternoon,
Toshio?

TOSHIO: I went shopping.

GLORIA: Did you buy a lot of things?

TOSHIO: No, not a lot . . . just a shirt for myself
and some gifts for my family. Look! I
bought this bracelet for my mother.

GLORIA: It's very pretty. What's it made of?
Silver?

TOSHIO: Yes. It's Mexican silver. And I
bought this silk scarf for my sister.

GLORIA: A silk scarf! Let me see. It's
beautiful! Hey, Toshio, look at
the label! Made in Japan!

TOSHIO: Oh, no! I don't believe it! I wanted to buy American gifts.

SAM: Don't worry, Toshio. You can exchange it tomorrow.

GLORIA: Don't forget to look at the labels next time. Japan exports a lot of
things to the United States, you know . . . cameras, radios . . .

SAM: Does Japan import anything,
Toshio?

TOSHIO: Of course it does! We import
copper, airplanes, food, and
many other things.

SAM: And what crops do you grow?

TOSHIO: Well, the main crops are tea
and rice. We also grow wheat,
but just in the northern part
of the country.

1 Vocabulary in Context 📼

Natural materials

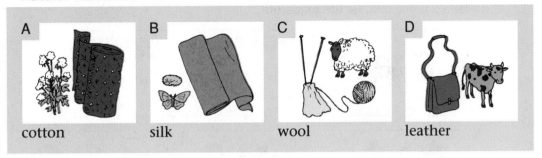

A: cotton B: silk C: wool D: leather

2 Practice

Prepare a statement about one thing you are wearing today. Then, go around the room and take turns saying what the person before you is wearing and what you are wearing.

> A: My jacket is made of wool.
> B: Monica's jacket is made of wool. My shirt is made of cotton.
> C: Dan's shirt is made of cotton. My blouse is made of cotton, too.
> Etc.

3 Presentation

Asking about materials

> GLORIA: Excuse me. **What's** this blouse **made of**?
> SALESPERSON: **It's made of** silk.
> GLORIA: **Is** the skirt **made of** silk, too?
> SALESPERSON: No, it isn't. **It's made of** cotton.

4 Practice

Work with a partner. Take turns asking and answering questions about the materials these clothes are made of.

A: What are these gloves made of?
B: Wool.
A: And is this hat made of wool, too?
B: Yes, it is.

1.    **2.**    **3.**

4.    **5.**    **6.**

5 Vocabulary in Context

Metals and jewelry

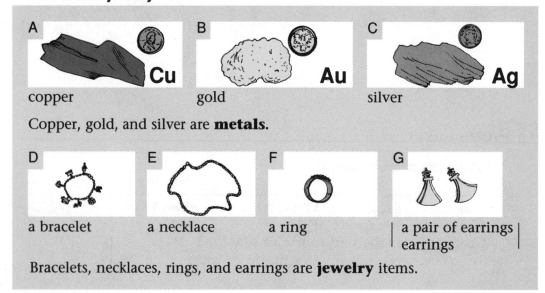

A **Cu** copper

B **Au** gold

C **Ag** silver

Copper, gold, and silver are **metals**.

D a bracelet   E a necklace   F a ring   G a pair of earrings / earrings

Bracelets, necklaces, rings, and earrings are **jewelry** items.

Giving detailed descriptions

> A noun used as an adjective goes **before** the noun it modifies.

1. Gloria has a bracelet.
   It's made of gold. ⟶ Gloria has a **gold bracelet**.
2. She has a scarf, too.
   It's made of silk. ⟶ She has a **silk scarf**, too.

7 **Practice**

Combine the two sentences, following the models.

> Sekila has two necklaces. They're made of gold.
>
> Sekila has two gold necklaces.

> Toshio is buying a pair of shoes. They're made of leather.
>
> Toshio is buying a pair of leather shoes.

1. Liz is buying a watch. It's made of gold.
2. Ted has a hat. It's made of wool.
3. That woman sells jewelry. It's made of copper.
4. I like that blouse. It's made of silk.
5. In Mexico I saw a lot of jewelry. It was made of silver.
6. They have boots for the winter. They're made of leather.
7. Colombia is famous for its rings. They're made of gold.
8. Adela is trying on a dress. It's made of cotton.
9. Cristina has some necklaces. They're made of silver.
10. I don't like that shirt. It's made of wool.

8 Presentation 📼

Talking about purchases

GLORIA: What did you do this afternoon, Toshio? TOSHIO: I went shopping. GLORIA: **Did** you **buy** a lot of things? TOSHIO: No, but I **bought** this silver bracelet.	The past tense of **buy** is **bought**.

9 Practice

Work with a partner. Take turns asking and answering questions about what you bought. Use these pictures and the conversation model in 8.

1.

4.

7.

2.

5.

8.

3.

6.

9.

10 Interaction

Pretend you bought two things at the mall. Write a description of the two things you bought; for example, *a gold ring and a pair of wool gloves.* Work with a partner and take turns guessing exactly what you each bought.

A: Did you buy a hat? B: No, I didn't. A: Did you buy a pair of gloves? B: Yes, I did. A: Are they made of leather? B: No, they aren't. A: Are they made of wool? B: Yes, they are.

11 Presentation

Asking for and giving information about where things are made

> GLORIA: **Was** that bracelet **made in** Mexico?
> CRISTINA: No, it wasn't. It **was made in** Colombia.

12 Practice

Do you know where any of the clothes you are wearing today were made? If so, point out the article of clothing to your classmates. They will try to guess the country of origin.

> A: Were those shoes made in Italy?
> B: No, they weren't.
> C: Were they made in Brazil?
> B: No, they weren't.
> D: Were they made in Spain?
> B: Yes, they were.

13 Presentation

Talking about imports and exports

> The present tense is used to talk about facts.

1. Japan **exports** cars **to** the United States.
2. Japan **imports** planes **from** the United States.

> SAM: What does Japan **export to** the United States?
> TOSHIO: Cars.
> SAM: And what does Japan **import from** the United States?
> TOSHIO: Airplanes.

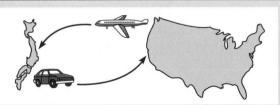

Pronounce these sentences.

1. England imports coffee, tea, and fruit.

2. Argentina imports cars, airplanes, and oil.

15 Practice

Study the chart. Take turns asking and answering questions about the trade between these countries. Use the conversation model in *13*.

Country	Imports	Imported from
United States		Venezuela
		Brazil
		Japan
		France
Japan		Saudi Arabia
		United States
		Colombia
Mexico		Germany
		United States
		United States
Venezuela		Italy
		United States
		Japan
Germany		Argentina
		Brazil
Brazil		Japan
		United States
		Saudi Arabia

> United States / import / Venezuela
> A: What does the United States import from Venezuela?
> B: Oil.

> United States / export / Venezuela
> A: What does the United States export to Venezuela?
> B: Computers.

1. Mexico / import / Germany
2. Argentina / export / Germany
3. Italy / export / Venezuela
4. Venezuela / import / Japan
5. France / export / United States

6. Japan / import / Colombia
7. Brazil / import / Saudi Arabia
8. Saudi Arabia / export / Japan
9. Brazil / import / Japan
10. Brazil / export / United States

16 Interaction

Work with a partner. Take turns making incorrect statements about the trade between the countries in the chart on page 54. Your partner will correct your statements.

> A: The United States exports cheese to France.
> B: No, it doesn't. It imports cheese from France.

17 Vocabulary in Context

Crops

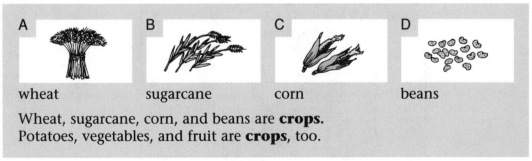

wheat   sugarcane   corn   beans

Wheat, sugarcane, corn, and beans are **crops**.
Potatoes, vegetables, and fruit are **crops**, too.

18 Presentation

Talking about a country's crops

> SAM: What does Japan grow, Toshio?
> TOSHIO: Japan grows tea and rice.

19 Practice

Work with a partner. Ask and answer questions about the crops of these countries. Use the conversation model in *18*.

Colombia	Mexico	Chile	China
coffee	coffee	wheat	rice
bananas	cotton	rice	wheat
rice	sugarcane	fruit	corn
corn	beans	corn	cotton
sugarcane	rice	beans	

20 Listening

Listen to the descriptions of these countries. Then complete the chart.

Country	Grows	Exports	Imports
Peru	corn	_____	_____
	_____	copper	computers
	_____	_____	
	coffee	coffee	
		_____	
		fish	
Costa Rica	_____	_____	_____
	bananas	_____	
	_____	meat	paper products
		sugar	
Italy	grapes	_____	_____
	_____	leather goods	wool
		_____	_____
		fruit	

56   Unit Five

21 Reading

Before You Read

1. Do you know where Thailand is?
2. What else do you know about Thailand?

Guide To Thailand

Location: Thailand is a beautiful country in southeast Asia.
Weather: It is very hot and rainy in July and August. From September through May it is dry, hot, and sunny, and there is a nice wind at times.
Crops: Rice and corn are very important, but sugarcane is also grown in many areas.
Products: Thailand makes beautiful silver jewelry and high-quality silk and cotton clothes.
Trade: There is a lot of trade with other countries.
Exports: Rice, corn, sugar, and silk and cotton clothes are the main exports.
Imports: Cars, oil, and metals are the main imports.

Comprehension

Now complete this paragraph about Thailand, using information from the guidebook.

Thailand is located in _____ . The weather in Thailand is _____ and _____ in _____ and _____ , but it is dry, hot, and sunny from _____ through _____ . Thailand grows _____ , _____ , and _____ . It makes beautiful silver jewelry and very pretty _____ and _____ clothes. Thailand exports _____ , _____ , _____ , and _____ . It has to import a lot of things, for example, cars, _____ , and _____ .

22 Writing

Write a paragraph about your own country. Answer these questions in your paragraph.

- Where is your country located?
- What is the weather like?
- What does your country grow?
- What does it make?
- What does it export?
- What does it import?
- What are some of its traditional foods?
- What are some of your country's important holidays?
- What is the most important year in your country's history? Why?

23 Final Activity

You and your partner meet on the street. Your partner tells you that he or she went shopping. Have a conversation about the things your partner bought.

A: Greet your friend.

B: Return greeting.

A: Ask your friend about this afternoon's activities.

B: Tell him or her.

A: Ask what he or she bought.

B: Tell him or her and show one of the gifts.

A: Comment on the gift. Ask what it is made of.

B: Give the information.

Continue the conversation.

COMMUNICATION
Talking about places to visit ▪ Explaining why places are famous ▪ Describing places ▪ Asking for and giving geographical information ▪ Asking about distance

GRAMMAR
Numbers from 120 to 99,000 ▪ *There are* ▪ Possessive adjective *its* ▪ Questions with *how* + adjective ▪ *How far is it from X to Y?*

SKILLS
Reading a map ▪ Reading a travel brochure ▪ Writing a descriptive paragraph

A Wonderful Trip!

Melanie Nava teaches English in Mexico City. She's talking to one of her students after class.

ALBERTO: Hi, Melanie. Did you have a good vacation?
MELANIE: Wonderful!
ALBERTO: Where did you go?
MELANIE: California, Arizona, New Mexico, Washington, D.C., New York . . .
ALBERTO: Really? What a long trip!
MELANIE: It certainly was.
ALBERTO: How far is it to New York from Arizona?
MELANIE: About 2,500 miles.
ALBERTO: And why did you go to Arizona?
MELANIE: Well, there are a lot of exciting places in Arizona, like the Grand Canyon. Arizona is famous for its deserts, too.

ALBERTO: Did you go to the Grand Canyon?
MELANIE: We sure did! What an experience! We went right down to the bottom.
ALBERTO: Did you walk down?
MELANIE: Oh no! It's too far. We went on mules.
ALBERTO: How deep is the canyon?
MELANIE: It's about 5,000 feet deep.
ALBERTO: Really? How long is it?
MELANIE: I think it's about 220 miles.
ALBERTO: How long is that in kilometers?
MELANIE: Well . . . It's about 350 kilometers.
ALBERTO: What a canyon! Did you take any pictures?
MELANIE: Yes, I did. I have them with me. Would you like to see them?

1 Presentation 🔲

Numbers from 120 to 99,000

120	one hundred (and) twenty / a hundred (and) twenty
135	one hundred (and) thirty-five
140	one hundred (and) forty
189	one hundred (and) eighty-nine
200	two hundred
256	two hundred (and) fifty-six
300	three hundred
417	four hundred (and) seventeen
500	five hundred
600	six hundred
700	seven hundred
800	eight hundred
900	nine hundred
1,000	one thousand / a thousand
6,000	six thousand
50,000	fifty thousand
99,000	ninety-nine thousand

1,500 = one thousand five hundred / fifteen hundred

2 Pronunciation 🔲

Pronounce these numbers.

123 one hundred twenty-three

200 two hundred

409 four hundred nine

1,000 one thousand

2,450 two thousand four hundred fifty

17,000 seventeen thousand

839 eight hundred thirty-nine

3 Practice

Read these numbers aloud to your partner.

a.	138	**d.**	591	**g.**	8,916	**j.**	11,614
b.	790	**e.**	2,823	**h.**	2,117	**k.**	17,382
c.	792	**f.**	4,559	**i.**	33,475	**l.**	85,265

4 Vocabulary in Context

Places to visit

A

This is a beach. It's in Puerto Rico.

B

This is a mountain. It's in Switzerland.

C

This is a temple. It's in India.

D

This is a pyramid. It's in Mexico.

E

This is a historic building. It's in Rome.

F

This is a wildlife park. It's in Kenya.

5 Presentation

Describing places with *there are*

A

ALBERTO:	Why did you go to Arizona?
MELANIE:	Because **there are** a lot of exciting places in Arizona.

B

ADELA:	Why would you like to visit Paris, Elinor?
ELINOR:	Because **there are** a lot of interesting museums in Paris.

6 Practice

Work with a partner. Take turns asking and giving reasons for visiting places.

Canada / beautiful mountains
A: Why would you like to visit Canada?
B: Because there are a lot of beautiful mountains in Canada.

1. Egypt / interesting pyramids
2. Thailand / wonderful temples
3. Brazil / great beaches
4. Washington / interesting museums
5. Kenya / exciting wildlife parks
6. Switzerland / high mountains
7. France / historic churches
8. California / fantastic beaches
9. India / beautiful temples
10. Greece / interesting historic buildings

7 Interaction

Work with a partner. Take turns giving a tourist advice about places to visit in your country.

A: I'm not busy next week. Where should I go?
B: You should go to _____ . There are a lot of
_____ in _____ .

8 Presentation 🔊

Yes/no questions with *there are*; short answers

Are	there	any rivers in Zaire?	Yes, there are.
			Yes, there's one.
		any deserts in Zaire?	No, there aren't.

GLORIA: Are there any mountains in Zaire, Sekila?
SEKILA: Yes, there are. There are a lot.
GLORIA: Are there any long rivers?
SEKILA: Yes, there's one, the Congo River.
GLORIA: And what about deserts? Are there any deserts?
SEKILA: No, there aren't.

9 Practice

Work with a partner. Take turns being a visitor to your partner's country. If you are from the same country, one of you can choose another country you know something about. Ask and answer questions about: *mountains, long rivers, deserts, lakes, beaches, wildlife parks*. Use the conversation model in *8*.

10 Presentation 🔊

Possessive adjective *its*

1. There are a lot of beautiful mountains and lakes in Canada. Canada is famous for **its** mountains and lakes.
2. Japan exports a lot of cars. Japan is famous for **its** cars.

11 Practice

Look at the pictures and say what each country is famous for.

Puerto Rico is famous for its beautiful beaches.

Puerto Rico

1.

Colombia

5.

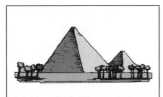

Italy

2.

Egypt

6.

Saudi Arabia

3.

France

7.

Thailand

4.

Costa Rica

8.

Kenya

12 Interaction

Working in groups, talk about what your country or places in your country are famous for. Talk about: *buildings, beaches, mountains, food, people, products, music, parks.*

New York City is famous for its tall buildings.
It is also famous for its food.

13 Vocabulary in Context

Describing places

Read the brochure. Look at the map to help you understand the new words.

The Colorado River

The Colorado River (1) **begins** its long trip in the (2) **high** Rocky Mountains in the state of Colorado.

From Colorado, the river (3) **flows** west into the desert in Utah. From Utah, it (4) **continues** its trip through the (5) **world-famous** Grand Canyon in Arizona. This beautiful canyon is 217 miles long, more than 4,921 feet deep and, at one point, 18 miles wide.

From Arizona, the Colorado River travels into Nevada (6) **through** Lake Mead. Then it turns south and flows along the (7) **border** between California and Arizona. The river finally (8) **ends** at the Gulf of California after a fascinating trip of 1,450 miles.

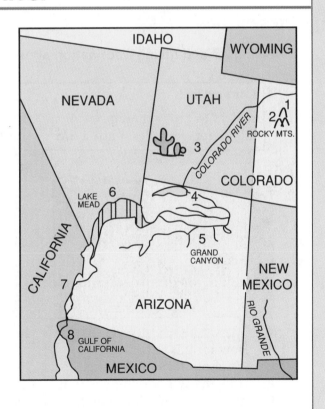

14 Practice

Describe the route of the Magdalena River by completing this text with: *flow, begin, continue, travel.* **Each verb may be used more than once.**

The Magdalena River (1) _____ its long trip in the south of Colombia. It (2) _____ east and then north through the towns of Neiva and Honda. It (3) _____ its journey north through Puerto Barrio and El Banco. At El Banco it (4) _____ west and then north again. It (5) _____ its journey in Barranquilla where it (6) _____ into the Caribbean Sea.

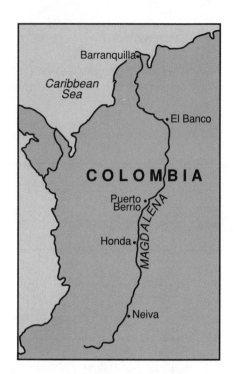

15 Presentation 🔲

Asking for and giving information about length, depth, width, and height

Conversions	
meters to feet = meters x 3.3	feet to meters = feet x .3048
kilometers to miles = km x 5/8	miles to kilometers = miles x 1.6

A
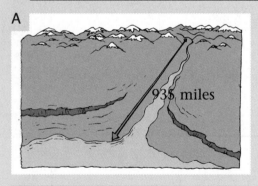

935 miles

B

2,145 feet

A:	How long is this river?
B:	It's about 935 miles long.
A:	How many kilometers is that?
B:	It's about 1,500 kilometers.

A:	How deep is this canyon?
B:	It's about 2,145 feet deep.
A:	How many meters is that?
B:	It's about 650 meters.

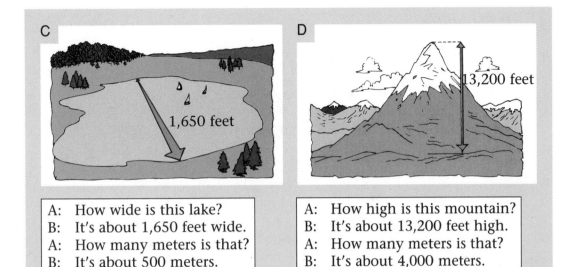

C	D
A: How wide is this lake?	A: How high is this mountain?
B: It's about 1,650 feet wide.	B: It's about 13,200 feet high.
A: How many meters is that?	A: How many meters is that?
B: It's about 500 meters.	B: It's about 4,000 meters.

16 Practice

Work with a partner. Ask and answer questions using *how*, as in *15*.

> the Nile River / 6,648 kilometers long
> A: How long is the Nile River?
> B: It's 6,648 kilometers long.
> A: How many miles is that?
> B: It's about 4,155 miles.

1. the Grand Canyon / more than 1,500 meters deep

2. the Mississippi River / 3,779 kilometers long

3. the Hudson River / about 500 meters wide

4. the Sahara Desert / 5,630 kilometers long

5. Mount Fuji / 3,776 meters high

6. the Amazon River / 5,440 kilometers long

7. Mount Everest / 8,848 meters high

8. Lake Mead / 12 kilometers wide

17 Presentation

Asking about distance

SEKILA: **How far is it** from New York to California?
GLORIA: **It's** about 2,750 miles.
SEKILA: And **how far is it** from New York to Atlanta?
GLORIA: **It's** about 840 miles.

18 Practice

Work with a partner. Student A works with Chart 1 and Student B with Chart 2.
Complete the missing information in your chart by asking your partner questions
with *How far . . . ?*

CHART 1

Number of Road Miles Between Some U.S. Cities

From	To Chicago	To Kansas City	To New York
Boston	994	1,391	_____
Los Angeles	2,054	_____	_____
Seattle	_____	_____	2,815
Washington, D.C.	671	_____	233

CHART 2

Number of Road Miles Between Some U.S. Cities

From	To Chicago	To Kansas City	To New York
Boston	_____	_____	206
Los Angeles	_____	1,585	2,786
Seattle	2,013	1,839	_____
Washington, D.C.	_____	1,043	_____

19 Reading

Before You Read

1. Do you like to travel?
2. Do you read travel brochures?
3. What kind of information do you find in travel brochures?

Pyramids of the Sun and Moon

Thirty-five miles north of Mexico City are the fabulous pyramids of the Sun and the Moon. Climb the narrow steps to the top of the 215-
5   foot-high Pyramid of the Sun and you will get a fantastic view of the whole site including the Avenue of the Dead, many temples and shrines, and the smaller Temple of the Moon.

Taxco

10 High in the hills of the southern Sierra Madre between Acapulco and Mexico City is
15 the delightful little town of Taxco. It is dominated by its superb, baroque church of Santa
20 Prisca and is a fascinating maze  of narrow streets where you'll find dozens of shops with all kinds of silver products.

Comprehension

A. Find a word:

1. in line 3 that means the same as *fantastic.*
2. in line 4 that is the opposite of *wide.*
3. in line 6 that means everything you can see from a place.
4. in line 10 that means the same as *high land.*
5. in line 15 that means the same as *wonderful.*
6. in line 18 that means almost the same as *excellent.*

B. Read the text again and answer the following questions:

1. How far is it from Mexico City to the pyramids of the Sun and the Moon?
2. How high is the Pyramid of the Sun?
3. What can you see from the top of the Pyramid of the Sun?
4. Where is Taxco located?
5. What three things is Taxco famous for?

20 Writing

A. The sentences below form a paragraph about Kenya, but they are not in the correct order. First put the sentences in order and then copy them as a paragraph.

___ Kenya's main crops are tea and coffee.

___ There are a lot of wonderful beaches and high mountains in Kenya, too.

___ It is famous for its wildlife parks.

___ Kenya is a beautiful country in East Africa.

___ Every year a lot of people go to Kenya to visit the wildlife parks.

___ It exports its very fine coffee to many European countries.

___ Mount Kenya, for example, is 17,058 feet high.

B. Now write a similar paragraph about your country.

Listening 🔲

Number your paper from 1-7. Listen to the description of Zaire. Then complete the sentences below.

1. There are a lot of _____ in Zaire.
2. It has a very long _____ , too.
3. Its name is the _____ .
4. It is about _____ miles long.
5. It flows into the _____ _____ .
6. Zaire's main crops are _____ and _____ .
7. Its exports are _____ and _____ .

22 **Final Activity**

Make two copies of the map below on a piece of paper. On one map give imaginary names to the mountains, the lakes, and the river. Complete other details, such as the height of the mountains. Then, working with a partner, find out all the information on his or her map. Ask questions like these:

What's the name of the mountain west of the lake?
And how high is it?

Fill out the second map with this information.

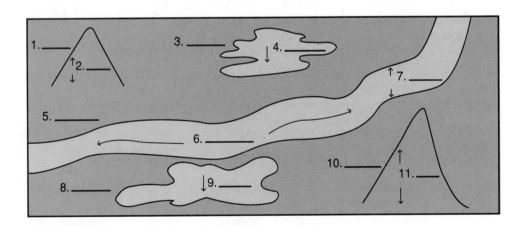

UNIT 7

COMMUNICATION
Talking about activities and chores ▪ Asking and telling about plans and intentions ▪ Making predictions ▪ Asking for and expressing an opinion or advice

GRAMMAR
Be + going to + infinitive ▪ Questions with *How often?* ▪ *Once, twice, three times* ▪ *I think . . .*

SKILLS
Taking notes ▪ Reading a travel schedule ▪ Writing a paragraph from notes

I'm Going to Be Busy

Mike stops by Bob's house. He rings the bell. Bob opens the door.

BOB: Hi, Mike. Come in.
MIKE: Thanks, Bob. I can't stay for long. I'm going to play basketball. Do you want to come?
BOB: Thanks, Mike, but not this morning. I'm going to be busy today.
MIKE: Really? What are you going to do?
BOB: I'm going to paint my room.
MIKE: Paint your room? Hey, that's a lot of work.
BOB: Yeah, it is. But you know what? I enjoy it.
MIKE: What color are you going to paint it?
BOB: White.
MIKE: White? That isn't very practical.
BOB: No, it isn't, but I like white. It's nice and bright.
MIKE: How often do you paint your room?
BOB: Once, sometimes twice a year.
MIKE: Twice a year! You sure like to paint!
BOB: Yeah, I do . . . Uh, is Ted going to play basketball, too?
MIKE: No, he's going to go running this morning . . . Well, I have to go now. See you at school Monday.

. . .

MIKE: Oh, no! Look at those clouds. It's going to rain again. That means no basketball.
BOB: Well, you can stay and help me paint my room then!
MIKE: That's an idea . . . but I think I should go home and clean my own room. It's a mess! See you later, Bob.
BOB: Thanks for stopping by, Mike.

72   **Unit Seven**

1 Vocabulary in Context 📼

Activities and chores

A

In his **free time,** Bob likes to **paint.** Today he is painting his room.

B

Elinor likes to **go for long walks** in her free time.

C

When Gloria has some free time, she likes to **practice** the guitar.

D

Adela likes to **sew** in her free time. Today she is making a blouse.

E

Mike likes to play basketball in his free time, but today he's going to **clean** his room.

2 Practice

Work with a partner. Ask and answer questions about the activities of the following characters from *Intercom 2000.*

Gino

A: What does Gino like to do in his free time?
B: He likes to swim, and he likes to read, too.

1.

Lisa

2.

Joyce

3.

Ted

4.

Tom

5.

Sekila

6.

Sam

---

3 Presentation 🔲

Asking about plans and intentions

> Use **be** + **going to** + *infinitive* to talk about future plans and intentions.

BOB:	Is Ted going to play basketball this morning?
MIKE:	No, he isn't. He's going to go for a walk.
BOB:	Is he going to stay home this afternoon?
MIKE:	Yes, he is.

4 Practice

Work with a partner. Ask and answer questions about Ted's, Adela's, and Gloria's plans and intentions for the coming weekend. Look at their "Things to Do" list.

Things to Do This Weekend			
	Ted	**Adela**	**Gloria**
Saturday afternoon	go to the library	clean the closets	paint the kitchen
Saturday night	go to the movies with Mike	make a blouse for Lisa	make a cake
Sunday morning	go for a walk	go to church	practice the guitar
Sunday afternoon	watch the football game	visit Elinor	go for a walk with Sekila

Ted / stay home / Saturday afternoon?
A: Is Ted going to stay home next Saturday afternoon?
B: No, he isn't. He's going to go to the library.

Ted / go to the movies / Saturday night?
B: Is Ted going to go to the movies next Saturday night?
A: Yes, he is.

1. Ted / study / Sunday morning?

2. Ted / watch TV / Sunday afternoon?

3. Adela / paint her bedroom / Saturday afternoon?

4. Adela / make a cake / Saturday night?

5. Adela / go to church / Sunday morning?

6. Adela / stay home / Sunday afternoon?

7. Gloria / paint the kitchen / Saturday afternoon?

8. Gloria / make a cake / Saturday night?

9. Gloria / practice the guitar / Sunday morning?

10. Gloria / stay home / Sunday afternoon?

5 Presentation 📼

Asking and telling about plans and intentions

> MIKE: What are you going to do this morning, Bob?
> BOB: I'm going to paint my room. And what are you going to do?
> MIKE: I'm going to play basketball.

6 Interaction

On a piece of paper write down what you intend to do: *after class today, next weekend, on your next vacation,* and *next year.* Work with a partner. Ask about each other's plans and intentions.

> A: What are you going to do _____ ?
> B: I'm going to _____ .
>   And what are you going to do?
> A: I'm going to _____ .

7 Presentation 📼

Questions with *How often . . . ?*

> To find out the number of times someone does something, ask:
>
> **How often** + | **do** | + subject + infinitive?
> | **does** |
>
> 1 time = **once**; 2 times = **twice**
> BUT: **three times, four times, five times**

> MIKE: How often do you paint your room, Bob?
> BOB: Once, sometimes twice a year.

> GLORIA: How often do you call your family, Sekila?
> SEKILA: Three or four times a month.

8 Practice

Work with a partner. Ask and answer questions about Bob's schedule.

WINFIELD HIGH SCHOOL CLASS SCHEDULE				*Bob Logan*	
Time	Monday	Tuesday	Wednesday	Thursday	Friday
8:10 AM	English	English	English	English	English
9:00 AM	Math	Math	Math	Math	Math
9:50 AM	Study Period	Art	Study Period	Art	Study Period
10:40 AM	Chemistry	Chemistry	Chemistry	Chemistry	Chemistry
11:30 AM	History	History	History	History	History
12:20 PM	Lunch	Lunch	Lunch	Lunch	Lunch
1:10 PM	French	French	French	French	French
2:00 PM	Soccer Practice	Basketball Practice	Basketball Practice	Soccer Practice	Soccer Practice

> math
> A: How often does Bob have math?
> B: Five times a week — on Monday, Tuesday, Wednesday, Thursday, and Friday.

1. English
2. a study period
3. chemistry
4. French
5. history
6. soccer practice
7. music
8. basketball practice
9. art

9 Interaction

Write on a piece of paper a list of the things you do regularly; for example, *go to the movies, clean your room, go for a long walk, study math, cook dinner, visit your grandparents*. Show your list to another student and ask each other how often you do each activity.

> A: How often do you _____ ?
> B: _____ . And how often do you _____ ?
> A: _____ .

10 Presentation 🔊

Making predictions

> To make a prediction, use **be** + **going to** + *infinitive*.

A

Look at those clouds. It's going to rain again.

B

Look at all that food. They're going to eat a lot.

11 Practice

Look at the pictures and make predictions about what will happen.

Elinor's going to go to bed early.

1.

2.

3.

4.

5.

6.

7.

8.

12 Listening

Number your paper from 1-8. Listen to this conversation between Gino and Sam. Take notes to complete the information.

1. Gino's plans for this afternoon: _____
2. Gino's plans for tomorrow: _____
3. Sam's plans for this afternoon: _____
4. Gino's prediction for this afternoon's weather: _____
5. Sam's plans for tonight: _____
6. Sam's prediction about the movie *Subway*: _____
7. Reason for his prediction: _____
8. Reason why Gino doesn't accept Sam's invitation: _____

13 Presentation

Expressing an opinion or giving advice

> BOB: Can you help me paint my room, Mike?
> MIKE: Sure! But **I think** you should clean it first. It's a mess!

14 Practice

Match the situations in 1-8 with the responses in *a-h*.

1. Do I have a fever?
2. Oh, no! It's raining, and I wanted to walk to the mall.
3. It's going to be a lovely afternoon.
4. Adela is feeling very nervous because she's working too hard.
5. Your room's a mess.
6. Does Lisa have a test tomorrow?
7. Bob always stays home on the weekends.
8. It's Tom's birthday next week.

a. I think he should go out more.
b. I think you should clean it.
c. Yes. I think she should study tonight.
d. I think we should go for a walk.
e. I think we should have a party for him.
f. Yes. I think you should go to bed.
g. I think you should drive.
h. I think she should relax more.

15 **Presentation**

Asking for an opinion or advice with *I think*

> GLORIA: What color **do you think** I should paint my room?
>   Yellow or light blue?
> SEKILA: I think you should paint it light blue. Yellow is too bright.

16 **Practice**

Take turns asking for and expressing an opinion.

> go / next summer? // Seattle or Miami?
> Seattle // Miami / hot
> A: Where do you think I should go next summer? Seattle or Miami?
> B: I think you should go to Seattle. Miami is too hot in the summer.

1. go / next December? // Atlanta or Anchorage?
   Atlanta // Anchorage / cold
2. time / call John? // at 7:00 AM or at 10:00 AM?
   at 10:00 AM // at 7:00 AM / early
3. color / paint my kitchen? // yellow or white?
   yellow // white / boring
4. go shopping / tonight? // the Riverview Mall or the Westlake Mall?
   the Riverview Mall // the Westlake Mall / far
5. take a vacation / this year? // March or July?
   July // March / rainy

17 **Reading**

Before You Read

1. Do you like to stay in one place
   when you are on vacation or do
   you like to travel around?
2. How do you like to travel on long
   trips? By train? By car? By bus?
   By plane or by boat?

Useful vocabulary:

1. £ = pound (British money)
2. An **itinerary** is a list of
   the places you will go and
   on what day.
3. To **transfer** means to go
   from one place to another.

USA West Coast

A marvelous 15 day tour

Your Itinerary

**Departures March 5th £795,
May 28th £849 &
October 1st £849**

☆ **Day 1**
Travel by bus from Norwich to London, Gatwick Airport, for your scheduled flight to **Los Angeles**. Transfer to **Hollywood**.

☆ **Day 2**
Free in **Hollywood** with opportunity to visit **Universal Studios, Beverly Hills**, and downtown **Los Angeles.**

☆ **Day 3**
Drive across **Los Angeles** for a full day visit to Disneyland. Then continue to **San Diego**.

☆ **Day 4**
Free in **San Diego** with city sightseeing tour followed by visit to **Tijuana** in **Mexico**.

☆ **Day 5**
Drive through the spectacular desert countryside to **Phoenix, Arizona.** Overnight stay at the fashionable resort of **Scottsdale**.

☆ **Day 6**
Free in **Scottsdale** to soak up the sunshine.

☆ **Day 7**
A leisurely drive into the green vegetation of **Northern Arizona.** Stop at **Montezuma's Castle** before continuing to **Flagstaff** for overnight stay.

☆ **Day 8**
Visit **Grand Canyon**, one of the greatest natural wonders of the world. Then continue to the gambling capital of **Las Vegas** - for a two night stay.

☆ **Day 9**
Free in **Las Vegas** - the 24 hour city!

☆ **Day 10**
Drive through the **Mojave Desert**. Overnight stay in **Fresno**.

☆ **Day 11**
Visit to **Yosemite National Park** with its 1,000 year old redwood trees. Then continue to **San Francisco** for a three night stay.

☆ **Days 12 & 13**
Free in **San Francisco**, with city sightseeing tour included!

☆ **Day 14**
Morning free prior to transfer to San Francisco Airport for return flight to London.

☆ **Day 15**
Morning arrival at London, Gatwick Airport. Bus back to Norwich.

TRAVELSPHERE
The Best in the West!
**Phone for our Brochure
0858 410456**

Comprehension

Answer the following questions based on the travel brochure.

1. Which part of the United States are the people on this tour going to visit?
2. How many of these tours are there in one year?
3. How are the people going to travel to the United States?
4. Which European city are they going to leave from?
5. If someone leaves on May 28th, how much is the tour going to cost?
6. Which American cities are they going to visit?
7. Which other places are they going to see?
8. Which other country are they going to visit?

18 Reentry

Complete this text with the following prepositions: *on, in, for, to, by, from.*

The Marshalls are a family from Cambridge, England. They are excited because on their next vacation they are going to go (1) _____ the United States. They are going to fly (2) _____ Gatwick Airport, London, (3) _____ Los Angeles. They are going to stay (4) _____ the U.S. (5) _____ fifteen days. During the tour they are going to visit a lot of interesting places. They are going to travel (6) _____ bus from one place to the next. They are leaving England (7) _____ March 5th. They want to go (8) _____ March because the weather is good then on the west coast of the U.S.

19 Writing

Write a paragraph describing Cristina's plans for next weekend. Use these notes from her diary.

Saturday ——————————————————	—————————————————— Sunday
- visit Sonia in Riverside - get bus at 10:30 AM - have lunch with Sonia - get bus to Winfield at 4:30 PM	- clean apartment - go for a walk with Gloria and Sekila in afternoon - see Gino in the evening

20 Final Activity

A. Move around the room. Ask your classmates questions to find out which of the following statements are true and which are false. Take notes.

A: Do you like to play tennis, Erik? B: Yes, I do.	**Useful vocabulary:** at least two = two or more

True or False?

1. More than three people like to play tennis. _____
2. All the students watched TV last night. _____
3. At least two students like to sew. _____
4. More than two students are going to visit another country this summer. _____
5. No students play the guitar. _____

B. Form groups of three. Share your information. Together, decide which statements are true and which are false.

UNIT 8

COMMUNICATION
Asking for and giving travel information •
Talking about past events • Making and
responding to polite requests

GRAMMAR
More irregular past tense • More Wh-
questions • Time expression + *ago* •
Could I . . . • Could you . . .

SKILLS
Taking notes • Reading a bus schedule •
Completing a letter

Have a Good Flight!

*Cristina is going to South America to visit her family. First she is going to visit her
aunt and uncle in Caracas. Then she is going to visit her parents in Bogota.
Cristina and Gino are at Kennedy Airport now. They left home very early because
Cristina is leaving on an early flight. They got to the airport an hour ago. First
Cristina went to the check-in counter.*

AGENT: Good morning, miss. May I see
your ticket?

CRISTINA: Here you are. Oh, could I have
a window seat, please?

AGENT: Certainly. Could you put your
baggage here, please?

A few minutes later.

AGENT: OK, miss. Your seat number is 20A. Your flight is boarding from
Gate 18 at 9:30. And there's one stopover in Miami.

CRISTINA: OK. How long do we stop in Miami?

AGENT: For two hours.

CRISTINA: Thanks a lot.

AGENT: You're welcome. Have a good flight!

1 Vocabulary in Context

Travel

A
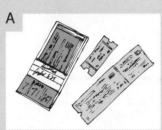

For a trip by plane, train, or bus, you need a **ticket**.

B

For a trip to another country you need a **passport**.

C

For a long trip you need a lot of | **baggage**. | **luggage**. |

D

For a short trip most people take only one | **suitcase**. | **bag**. |

E

The **agent** at the **check-in counter** gives you your **seat number**.

F

You **board** an airplane from a **gate**.

2 Practice

Complete the conversations with one of the travel words from 1.

1. A: Do you have a lot of _____ , sir?
   B: No, I just have these two bags.
2. A: Excuse me. Where do I board Flight 407 for Miami?
   B: At _____ 42.
3. A: What's your _____ ?
   B: 21C. It's a window seat.
4. A: Excuse me. Where can I buy a _____ ?
   B: Over there at the ticket counter.
5. A: Do I have to show my passport at the check-in counter?
   B: I'm not sure. Why don't you ask the _____ ?

Presentation 🔲

Talking about past events

BOB:	Cristina and Gino **left** at 6:30 yesterday morning.
MIKE:	Why **did** they **leave** so early?
BOB:	Because Cristina **had to** be at the airport at 8:30.
MIKE:	What time **did** her flight **leave**?
BOB:	At 9:30, and she **got to** Caracas at 4:30.

Present	Past
leave	left
have to	had to
get to	got to

---

4 **Practice**

Complete the following paragraph with the past tense of: *meet, get to, be, drive, have, have to, go, leave.* Some verbs are used more than once.

Cristina (1) _____ a very busy day yesterday. Gino (2) _____ Cristina at her house at 6:30. They (3) _____ to the airport in Gino's car. They (4) _____ the airport at 7:30. First they (5) _____ to the check-in counter. Then they (6) _____ breakfast. Cristina's flight (7) _____ at 9:30. Gino didn't wait at the airport because he (8) _____ be at the Roma at 11:30. Cristina (9) _____ Caracas at 4:30 PM. It (10) _____ a very long day.

---

5 **Reentry**

Simple past tense: interrogative, negative, and affirmative

Complete this conversation with *did or didn't*, or with the infinitive or the past tense of: *get to, have, have to, leave, meet, be.*

Why __*did*__ Cristina go to Caracas? To visit her aunt and uncle.

1. How _____ Cristina get to Caracas?
   She flew.
2. How did Cristina _____ the airport?
   By car.

3. What time _____ she leave home?
At 6:30.

4. Where did she and Gino _____ breakfast?
At the airport.

5. Did Cristina have a big breakfast?
No, she didn't. She _____ too excited.

6. Did Gino wait with Cristina at the airport?
No, he _____ . He _____ be in Winfield at 11:30.

7. What time did Cristina's flight leave?
It _____ New York at 9:30, and it _____ Caracas at 4:30.

8. Did Cristina's uncle meet her at the airport in Caracas?
Yes, he did, and her aunt _____ her, too.

6 Presentation

Information questions: *how long* and *who* (direct object)

A
CRISTINA:	**How long** do we stop in Miami?
CLERK:	For two hours.

Useful vocabulary:

Your **aunt** is your mother's or father's sister.
Your **uncle** is your mother's or father's brother.

B
GLORIA:	**Who** did you visit in Caracas, Cristina?
CRISTINA:	My aunt and uncle.

1. To find out the number of hours, weeks, years, etc., ask **How long** . . . ?

Question					Answer	
	do	we	stop	here?	For two hours.
How long	did	Gino	wait	at the airport?	For half an hour.

2. Questions with **Who** as direct object

Question				Answer
		Cristina	visit?	Her aunt and uncle.
Who	did	Gino	take to the airport?	Cristina.

7 Practice

Work with a partner. Ask and answer questions using the chart below.

> A: Who did Gloria visit last summer?
>
> B: Her aunt in New York City.
>
> A: How long did she stay at her aunt's house?
>
> B: For three days.

Name	When	People Visited	Length of Visit
Gloria	last summer	aunt in New York City	three days
the Navas	in 1990	the Youngs	one week
Adela	last Sunday	Elinor	two hours
Cristina	last month	her parents	one week
Mike	last week	a friend in Westlake	two days
Howard	last weekend	an uncle in Chicago	one day

8 Interaction

On a piece of paper write when you made five visits in the past; for example, last night, last Sunday. Work with a partner and exchange lists. Take turns asking and answering questions about these visits.

> A: Who did you visit ___last week___ ?
>
> B: ___My sister___ .
>
> A: And how long did you stay ___at your sister's house___ ?
>
> B: ___Two hours___ .

Presentation 🔲

Time expression + *ago*

1. Today is Sunday. Cristina got to Caracas on Friday. She got there **two days ago.**
2. Today is October 10th. Toshio came here on September 10th. He came here **a month ago.**

10 Practice

Read the following situations.   Then make sentences using time expressions + *ago*.

> It's 10:30 PM. The Logans had dinner at 6:30.
>
> The Logans had dinner four hours ago.

1. Today is Thursday. We saw the movie on Monday.
2. This is October. Sam was in New York City in May.
3. It's 8:45. Mike came home at 8:30.
4. This is Monday, April 25th. I took this picture on Monday, April 11th.
5. This is August. Mike was in Mexico last August.
6. It's 3:00 PM. I had lunch at 1:00 PM.
7. It's 1991. Mike was in Mexico City in 1989.
8. It's June 10th. Mike saw Toshio on June 3rd.
9. This is March. The baby was born in January.
10. It's September 16th. Kim went to the beach with her family on September 2nd.

11 Interaction

On a piece of paper write a list of five past actions or events; for example, *started this course, got my first job.* Exchange lists with a partner. Interview each other about when you did everything.

> A: When did you _____ ?
> B: _____ ago.

12 Presentation

Making and responding to polite requests (1)

Use **Could I . . . ?** when you're asking for something.

A

CRISTINA: Could I have a window seat, please?

AGENT: Yes, of course. Could I see your ticket, please?

CRISTINA: | Here it is. | | Here you are. |

B

AGENT: Could I see your ticket, please?

SEKILA: I'm afraid I can't find it.

13 Practice

Work with a partner. Take turns making and responding to polite requests in the following situations.

A: You want to read a newspaper during a flight.
YOU SAY: Could I have a newspaper, please?

B: You don't have any newspapers today.
YOU SAY: I'm afraid we don't have any newspapers today.

1. A: You need to have someone's address.
   B: You give your address.
2. A: You need to have someone's telephone number.
   B: You explain politely that you don't have a telephone.
3. A: You work at an airport. You need to look at someone's baggage.
   B: You respond politely in the affirmative.
4. A: You're at a ticket counter. You want two tickets to Miami.
   B: You respond politely in the affirmative.
5. A: You're at a ticket counter. You want to change the time of your flight to Seattle from the morning to the afternoon.
   B: You explain politely that there aren't any afternoon flights to Seattle.

14 Presentation

Making and responding to polite requests (2)

Use **Could you . . . ?** when you want someone to do something for you.

AGENT: Could you put your baggage here, please?
CRISTINA: Of course.
Sure.

15 Practice

Work with a partner. Take turns making and responding to polite requests in the following situations.

You're on a bus. It's very hot. What do you say to the person in the window seat?
A: Could you open the window, please?
B: Of course.

1. You work at an airport. You want to look inside a traveler's suitcase. What do you say to the traveler?
2. You have to write down a person's last name, but you can't spell it. What do you say to him or her?
3. You didn't hear the last letter of his or her last name. How do you ask him or her to repeat it?
4. You have a lot of things in your hands. You can't open a door. What do you say to a friend?
5. You are a teacher. The students are writing an exercise. You have to stop the class now. What do you say to your students?

16 Listening

Listen to the conversations. Complete the information that you hear about each passenger.

Passenger 1
a. She wants to travel by ____ .
b. She is going to ____ .
c. She has to be there at ____ .
d. She asks about ____ , too.

Passenger 2
a. He is leaving from ____ .
b. He got on the bus to ____ .
c. He wants to go to ____ .
d. His bus leaves at ____ .

17 Reading

Before You Read

1. When do you use a bus or a train schedule?
2. What kind of information do you find in these schedules?

STANDARD SYMBOLS

f — Flag stop. Bus will stop on signal to receive and
    discharge passengers.

☕ — Rest stop.

✗ — Meal or lunch stop.

ST. PETERSBURG—CLEARWATER—TAMPA—LAKELAND—WINTER HAVEN

READ DOWN

	1004	3797	1114	1232	3668	1092	3738	1165	1008	1094	3684	3707	1168	3794
Folder No. 115 **170** FREQUENCY →	AM				→	PM								→
ST. PETERSBURG, FL 🚌 .... (172–177) Lv	5 50	6 45	7 35	10 05	....	1 00	2 25	....	3 30	4 45	6 30	....	11 40	....
Seminole...............	↓	↓		10 30	....	↓	↓	....	↓	5 10	↓	....	↓	....
Clearwater 🚌 .... (167–172–177)	6 20	7 15	↓	↓	....	1 30	↓	1 20	4 00	5 40	7 00	11 35	↓	....
Tampa Airport ②	↓	↓			....	↓		1 45	↓	↓	7 25	↓	↓	....
Tampa 🚌 .... Ar	6 50	☕7 45	8 10	11 10	....	☕2 00	3 00	2 00	✗4 30	6 15	☕7 40	12 05	12 15	→
Tampa 🚌 Lv	7 00	8 00	....	....	11 30	2 20	3 10	←	5 00	....	8 05	....	....	12 30
Tampa *East*	↓	↓	....	....	11 40	↓	3 30	....	↓	....	↓	....	....	↓
Plant City	7 30	8 30	....	....	12 10	↓	....	....	5 35	....	8 40	....	....	1 05
Lakeland 🚌 (LB) .... Ar	8 00	9 00	....	....	12 35	3 05	....	....	6 00	....	Ⓛ9 05	....	....	Ⓛ1 25
Auburndale.................................	f	↓	....	....	f	↓	....	....	f	....	↓	....	....	↓
WINTER HAVEN, FL 🚌 (LB) .... Ar	8 35	9 30	....	....	1 10	3 40	....	....	6 35	....	Ⓛ9 35	....	....	Ⓛ1 55

Comprehension

1. How many buses leave St. Petersburg for Winter Haven every day?

2. How many leave in the morning and how many leave in the afternoon or at night?

3. Which buses have a rest stop? Give their schedule numbers.

4. Do any of the buses have a meal stop? Give the schedule number(s).

5. How long is the trip from St. Petersburg to Winter Haven on Bus 1004?

6. How long does Bus 3797 stop in Tampa?

18 Reentry

Questions with *what, what time, how long*

Work with a partner. One of you is a bus driver and the other is a passenger. Take turns asking and answering questions about Buses 3797, 1092, 1008, and 3684 in the schedule in *17.*

PASSENGER:	Excuse me. What time does Bus 1004 leave St. Petersburg?
BUS DRIVER:	At 5:50.
PASSENGER:	And what's the first stop?
BUS DRIVER:	Clearwater.
PASSENGER:	How long do you stop in Tampa?
BUS DRIVER:	For 10 minutes.
PASSENGER:	And what time does the bus get to Winter Haven?
BUS DRIVER:	8:35.

19 Writing

After Caracas, Cristina went to Bogota. From there she wrote to Gino. Use the notes from her diary to complete her letter.

DIARY

FRIDAY
- left New York, 9:30
- got to Caracas, 4:30
- Uncle Leo and Aunt Teresa met me at airport

SATURDAY
- tired; rested all day

SUNDAY
- morning: sightseeing
- lunch: restaurant
- afternoon: visited friends
- 12 midnight: left for Bogota

Bogota, Colombia
October 10, 1990
Dear Gino,
    I hope you had a good trip back to Winfield.
I had a great time in Caracas. I arrived _____
_____
    On Saturday I was very tired so _____
_____
    On Sunday morning _____
and at lunchtime _____
In the afternoon _____
Then at midnight _____
My parents met me at the airport. They
look wonderful.
    How are things in Winfield? Say hello
to everyone, and write soon. I miss you.
                            Love, Cristina

20 Final Activity

Think about a trip you took recently. Your teacher will ask you the following
questions about your trip:

1. Where did you go?
2. Who did you go with?
3. How did you get there?
4. How long did it take you?
5. What is special about the place you visited?
6. What was an interesting thing that you did there?

Listen to question #1 and write your answer on a piece of paper. Then fold the
paper, so that the other students can't see what you wrote. Now, give the paper to
a student on your right.

Follow the same procedure for questions #2-6, writing your answer on the piece
of paper from your classmate. When you are finished, unfold the paper and read
the story. Is it funny? Share your story with a small group of students or with the
class.

COMMUNICATION
Expressing dissatisfaction ▪ Talking about occupations ▪ Explaining wishes or desires ▪ Asking for additional information ▪ Talking about ability ▪ Describing personal qualities

GRAMMAR
Contrasting *would like to* + verb with *like to* + verb ▪ *What else?* ▪ *Know how to* + verb

SKILLS
Writing a paragraph ▪ Reading a job ad

I'm Bored with My Job

Sekila meets Liz at Nelson's Coffee Shop.

SEKILA: Hi, Liz!

LIZ: Oh, hi, Sekila!

SEKILA: You don't look very happy. What's the matter?

LIZ: Oh, I don't know. I guess I'm bored with my job.

SEKILA: But international telephone operators get good pay and benefits.

LIZ: Yeah, but I have to sit in one place all day. I hate it.

SEKILA: Well, what do you want to do?

LIZ: I don't know, but I like to work with people.

SEKILA: You're good at languages. Would you like to be a bilingual secretary?

LIZ: Not really. I don't know how to type.

SEKILA: Well, let's see. You can't type, but you're good at languages, and you like to work with people. What else do you like to do?

LIZ: I like to travel.

SEKILA: Wait a minute! I just saw an ad in the paper . . . Yes, here it is. This would be a great job for you, Liz!

1 Presentation 🔲

Expressing dissatisfaction

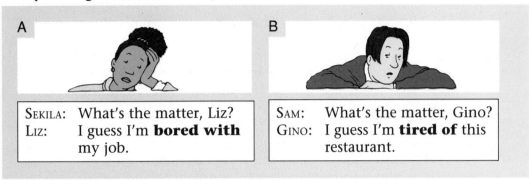

A	B
SEKILA: What's the matter, Liz? LIZ: I guess I'm **bored with** my job.	SAM: What's the matter, Gino? GINO: I guess I'm **tired of** this restaurant.

2 Pronunciation 🔲

A. Pronounce the questions and answers.

1. What's the matter?

   I don't know. I guess I'm bored with my job.

2. What's the matter?

   I don't know. I guess I'm tired of this city.

B. Now practice these sentences with the same intonation.

1. I guess I'm bored with this town.
2. I guess I'm tired of this weather.
3. I guess I'm bored with these people.
4. I guess I'm tired of this food.
5. I guess I'm bored with this place.
6. I guess I'm tired of my job.

3 Interaction

Talk to a few classmates. Take turns finding out about each other's dissatisfaction with something. Use real or imaginary things. Then tell the class what you learned about your classmate.

A: Hi, _____ ! You don't look very happy. What's the matter?
B: Oh, I don't know. I guess I'm _____ .

4 Reentry

Occupations

Match the following occupations with the descriptions in 1-10.

a. cook   **e.** homemaker   **h.** high school student
b. waitress   **f.** mechanic   **i.** travel agent
c. nurse   **g.** electrician   **j.** flight attendant
d. actor

1. This person goes to high school.
2. This person helps people with their travel arrangements.
3. This person takes care of the children and the house.
4. This person fixes lights, television sets, and radios.
5. This is a woman, and she serves the food in a restaurant.
6. This person prepares the food in a restaurant.
7. This is a man, and he acts in movies and plays.
8. This person fixes cars.
9. This person serves the food and helps the passengers on an airplane.
10. This person helps doctors with their work.

5 Vocabulary in Context

More occupations

 A **bank teller** works with money.

 A **farmer** grows fruit and vegetables.

 A **lawyer** helps people with their legal problems.

 A **carpenter** makes things with wood.

 A **firefighter** fights fires.

 A **journalist** writes for newspapers and magazines.

G A **letter carrier** delivers mail to your home.

 H A **computer programmer** writes programs for computers.

 I A **secretary** types letters and reports.

 J A **receptionist** greets people and answers the telephone.

6 Practice

Match the occupations in *5* with the descriptions below.

1. This person has to be very good in math.
2. This person has to walk a lot.
3. This person's business is growing food.
4. This person is often the first person you talk to in a company or a hotel.
5. This person writes about interesting people and events.
6. Usually this person has to get to a place very fast.
7. This person helps people with their problems with the law.
8. This person makes things with his or her hands.

7 Presentation

Contrasting *would like to + verb* with *like to + verb*

> Use **would like to + verb** to *express* wishes or desires.
> Use **like to + verb** to *explain* wishes or desires.

A
SEKILA: What **would you like to** do, Liz?
LIZ: I don't know, but **I like to** work with people and **I like to** travel.

B
ADELA: Where **would Elinor like to** go on her next vacation?
HOWARD: Paris.
ADELA: Why **would she like to** go to Paris?
HOWARD: Because **she likes to** go to museums and **she likes to** go shopping. **She doesn't like to** lie on the beach all day.

Work with a partner. Ask and answer questions about why the following people wish to do these things.

> Mike / be / doctor // sick people
> A: Why would Mike like to be a doctor?
> B: Because he likes to work with sick people.
>
> Bob / New York City / bus // travel by train
> A: Why would Bob like to go to New York City by bus?
> B: Because he doesn't like to travel by train.

1. Ted / be / lawyer // work with people
2. Joyce / mechanic // fix things
3. Liz / change / job // sit in one place all day
4. Lisa / live / New York City // live in a small town
5. Mike / buy / car // drive
6. Adela / get / job // stay home all day
7. Mike / go / Mexico again // speak Spanish
8. Elinor / go / Chinese restaurant next Sunday // cook on the weekend
9. Howard / stay / home next vacation // travel a lot
10. Tom / stay / home next weekend // work in the yard

9 **Presentation**

Asking for additional information

A
> SEKILA: You like to work with people. **What else** do you like to do?
> LIZ: I like to travel.

B
> BEN: I can speak three languages.
> NICK: Really? **What else** can you do?
> BEN: I can type.

C
> CUSTOMER: We'd like a mushroom pizza.
> WAITER: OK . . . and **what else** would you like?
> CUSTOMER: A salad and some bread.

10 Practice

Use *What else?* to ask for more information about the following people.

> A: Cristina can type well.
> B: ___*What else can she do?*___
> A: She can cook well, too.

1. A: Gloria can play the guitar very well.
 B: _____ ?
 A: She sings well, too.

2. A: Gino can make the Roma sauce.
 B: _____ ?
 A: He can make pizza, too.

3. A: The Youngs have a lot of books.
 B: _____ ?
 A: They have a lot of records, too.

4. A: Joyce likes basketball.
 B: _____ ?
 A: She likes tennis, too.

5. A: Sam plays soccer.
 B: _____ ?
 A: He plays baseball, too.

6. A: Bob enjoys English and history.
 B: _____ ?
 A: He enjoys music, too.

7. A: Ted had steak and salad for lunch.
 B: _____ ?
 A: He had some ice cream, too.

8. A: Toshio bought a scarf.
 B: _____ ?
 A: He bought some jewelry, too.

9. A: Sekila likes to go shopping.
 B: _____ ?
 A: She likes to go to the marina, too.

10. A: Lisa had to wash the breakfast dishes yesterday.
 B: _____ ?
 A: She had to cook dinner, too.

11 Interaction

Look at the list of activities and write down at least two of your preferences for each one. Then use the model to find out about a classmate's preferences.

Activities	
1. eat	**6.** do at lunch hour
2. read	**7.** do in a big city
3. watch on TV	**8.** do in the country
4. do on the weekends	**9.** listen to on the radio
5. do on vacation	**10.** buy when you go shopping

A: What do you like to ___eat___ , Jim?
B: _____Fruit and vegetables_____ .
A: And what else do you like to ___eat___ ?
B: _Fish_ .

12 Presentation

Talking about ability

To talk about ability, use **know how to** + *verb*.

SEKILA: Would you like to be a bilingual secretary?
LIZ: Not really. I **don't know how to** type.
SEKILA: Would you like to be a flight attendant?
LIZ: Yes, I think I would. I **know how to** speak three foreign languages, and I like to travel.

13 Practice

Work with a partner. Take turns asking and answering questions about your preferences and abilities for these professions.

> a farmer // grow fruit and vegetables
>
> A: Would you like to be a farmer?

> B: Not really. I don't know how to grow fruit and vegetables.

> B: Yes, I think I would. I know how to grow fruit and vegetables.

1. a computer programmer // write programs
2. a mechanic // fix cars
3. a cook // make good food
4. an architect // plan buildings
5. a secretary // type well
6. an artist // draw well
7. a journalist // write interesting articles
8. a homemaker // cook and take care of a home
9. a lawyer // answer legal questions
10. a carpenter // make things with wood

14 Vocabulary in Context

Describing personal qualities

1. Ted likes to help people. He listens to their problems. He is very **caring**.
2. Gloria likes to meet and talk to new people. She is **outgoing**.
3. Sam fixes cars. He doesn't work fast because his work isn't easy. Sam has to be very **careful**.
4. Tom answers a lot of questions at the travel agency. Sometimes he answers the same question again and again, and he is always polite. Tom is very **patient**.
5. Lisa likes to make things. She makes beautiful clothes and interesting food. Lisa is **creative**.
6. Elinor works a lot. She is never tired. Elinor is **energetic**.

15 Practice

Use words from *14* and other words you know to describe the personal qualities of people in the professions described below.

> A doctor works with sick people.
>
> A doctor has to be very caring.

1. A pilot's job isn't easy.

2. A receptionist talks to a lot of people.

3. A teacher answers the same questions again and again.

4. A computer programmer shouldn't work fast.

5. A carpenter makes beautiful things.

6. A letter carrier sometimes walks a lot every day.

7. A flight attendant meets and talks to a lot of people.

8. Sometimes a farmer works from 6:00 AM to 10:00 PM.

16 Listening

Number your paper from 1-10. Listen to the conversation. Then read the statements and write *True, False,* or *I don't know* for each one.

1. Sekila is creative.

2. Sekila is caring.

3. Sekila knows how to play the piano.

4. Gloria is creative.

5. Gloria is patient.

6. Sekila is patient.

7. Gloria wants to be a teacher.

8. Gloria is energetic.

9. Sekila is going to be a lawyer.

10. Sekila knows how to talk to people.

17 Writing

Choose a profession you would like to have and one you wouldn't like to have. Write two paragraphs explaining why you would and wouldn't like to have each profession. Add two sentences of your own to each of the paragraphs below.

I would like to be a _____ because I like to _____ and because I know how to _____ . I have the right qualities for this profession. I am _____ and _____ .

I would not like to be a _____ because I don't know how to _____ and I don't like to _____ . I don't have the right personal qualities for this profession. I am not _____ or _____ .

18 Reading

Before You Read

1. Do you ever look at the job ads in the newspaper?
2. What kind of information is given in a job ad?

DRIVERS

We are a nationwide trucking co. in a new terminal in Stoneham, MA. Seeking Class 1 Drivers for local and road work. Excellent salary and benefits. Interested applicants call:
1–800–445–1115

OVERNITE

95 Oak Street
Stoneham, MA 02180
Equal Opportunity Employer

AUTO MECHANICS WANTED!

- Top pay
- Vacations
- Schooling
- Immediate opening
Apply Service Department

NORTH END CHEVROLET, INC.
Telephone 894–6000

NORTH END
CHEVROLET

110 MAIN ST.,
WALTHAM
894–6000

Receptionist
Full Time

Our editorial department is seeking a receptionist for our Livonia office. Must have good telephone manners and an ability to deal with the public.

You will need: typing 55 wpm, word processing, filing and good organizational skills. High school diploma or equivalent, two years receptionist experience, preferably with a newspaper. Apply in person.

THE
Observer & Eccentric
NEWSPAPERS, INC

36251 SCHOOLCRAFT
LIVONIA, MICHIGAN 48151–0428
An Equal Opportunity Employer

Comprehension

Copy the chart below. Then complete it for each ad.

	Ad 1	Ad 2	Ad 3
Type of occupation:			
Name of company:			
Type of experience or qualifications (if any):			
Benefits (if any):			
To get more information:			

19 Final Activity

A. Work with a partner. Imagine that you are both looking for a job. Look at the list of job openings and help each other decide which jobs are best for you. Talk about what you like to do and know how to do. Also talk about your personal qualities.

JOB OPENINGS

receptionist
teacher's aide, math or history
letter carrier
computer programmer
cook
mechanic

B. Write three sentences about which job you chose and why. Share your sentences with the class.

COMMUNICATION
Talking about interviews and résumés ▪
Reporting what someone said

GRAMMAR
How long vs. *when* ▪ *From . . . until* ▪
Preposition: *during* ▪ Direct and indirect
speech

SKILLS
Reading a résumé ▪ Taking notes during a
phone call ▪ Writing a short report based on
notes ▪ Reading a newspaper article ▪
Writing a résumé

A Job Interview

*Ellen Roberts, the personnel manager for Worldwide Airlines, is interviewing Liz.
She is looking at Liz's résumé.*

MS. ROBERTS: I see you attended the Winfield
Language Institute, Ms. Young.

LIZ: Yes. I studied French and
Spanish there.

MS. ROBERTS: Oh, and I see that you went to
Germany. How long were you
there?

LIZ: Let me see . . . uh, for five months.

MS. ROBERTS: And when were you there?

LIZ: I was there from April until September, 1987.

MS. ROBERTS: Tell me about your stay in Germany. What did you do there?

LIZ: Well, during my stay in Bonn, I lived with a German family. I
helped with the housework and the children, and I studied
German.

MS. ROBERTS: That's interesting. I see that currently you're an international
telephone operator. Why do you want to leave that job?

LIZ: Well, I liked being an operator very much at first, because I
used my languages a lot. But now my job isn't very
challenging, and it's too mechanical.

MS. ROBERTS: And why would you like to be a flight attendant?

LIZ: Because I like people. I like to travel, too, and I know four
languages.

MS. ROBERTS: Well, Ms. Young, you certainly have the kind of experience
we're looking for. But, I have a lot of applicants for this
position and we're interviewing all this week. We'll call you
next week, OK?

LIZ: That would be fine.

MS. ROBERTS: It was nice meeting you, Ms. Young.

LIZ: Nice meeting you, too, Ms. Roberts.

Interviews and résumés

Liz Young is an **applicant** for a job as a flight attendant. She called Ms. Roberts to make an **appointment** for an **interview**. She sent Ms. Roberts her **résumé** before the interview. Ms. Roberts **interviewed** Liz today.

RÉSUMÉ

```
Elizabeth Young
10 South Kennedy Avenue
Winfield, New York 11500
Telephone: (516) 866-4715
```

EDUCATION

1987–1989	Winfield Modern Language Institute, Winfield, N.Y.
1982–1986	Winfield High School, Winfield, N.Y.

EXPERIENCE

1989–present	International telephone operator for Winfield Telephone Company, Winfield, N.Y.
June, 1988–September, 1988	Waitress at the French Restaurant, Winfield, N.Y.
September, 1986–April, 1987	Nurse's aide at New York Hospital, New York, N.Y.
June, 1986–August, 1986	Waitress at the Roma Restaurant, Winfield, N.Y.

TRAVEL

April–September, 1987	Germany

LANGUAGES Excellent German and French, fair Spanish

REFERENCES

```
Jose Garcia, Director,
   Winfield Modern Language Institute
Mary Fisher, Principal,
   Winfield High School
Toshio Ito, Flight Attendant,
   Japan Air Lines
```

2 Practice

Complete the following conversation using one of these words:
education, nurse's aide, job ad, interview, appointment, experience, applicants.

MIKE: How was the (1) _____ , Liz?

LIZ: It was OK, but there are a lot of (2) _____ .

MIKE: Don't worry about it, Liz. Look! Did you see this (3) _____ for a bilingual secretary?

LIZ: Yes, I did.

MIKE: Are you going to make a/an (4) _____ for a/an (5) _____ for this job, too?

LIZ: I don't think so. I don't have the right kind of (6) _____ .

MIKE: But you have a good (7) _____ and you can speak four languages.

LIZ: That's true. But I can't type, and I don't have any office experience.

MIKE: Didn't you work in an office one summer?

LIZ: No, I worked as a/an (8) _____ at the hospital.

MIKE: Oh, yeah. That's right.

3 Presentation

Prepositions: *from . . . until . . .*

> Use **from . . . until . . .** to show when something begins and ends.

> MS. ROBERTS: How long were you in Germany?
> LIZ: For five months.
> MS. ROBERTS: And when were you there?
> LIZ: I was there **from** April **until** September, 1987.

4 Practice

Use information from Liz's résumé on page 106 to ask and answer questions with *how long* and *when*.

> work / Roma
>
> A: How long did Liz work at the Roma?
> B: For two months.
> A: And when did she work there?
> B: She worked there from June until August, 1986.

1. work / New York Hospital
2. study / German
3. work / French Restaurant
4. study / Winfield Modern Language Institute

5 Interaction

On a piece of paper, write down five important events in your life; for example, *I started high school, I went to New York, I started my job.* Work with a partner. Look at his or her list of events and ask at least two questions about each event. Use the questions *How long* and *When did/were you . . . ?* when appropriate.

When you are finished, tell the class about one very interesting event on your partner's list.

6 Presentation

Preposition: *during*

ToSHIO: When did you work for a family?
LIZ: **During** my stay in Germany.

SEKILA: How are you feeling, Liz?
LIZ: I'm OK now, but I was very nervous **during** the interview.

7 Practice

Work with a partner. Take turns asking questions about the people in 1-10 and giving the answers from *a-j*. Use the past tense.

> Liz / nervous?
> A: When was Liz nervous?
> the interview with Ms. Roberts last week
> B: During the interview with Ms. Roberts last week.

1. Ted / bored?
2. Melanie / see her parents?
3. Sam / work hard?
4. Bob / nervous?
5. rain a lot / in Winfield?
6. the students / bored?
7. Toshio / very busy?
8. Cristina / see a lot of friends?
9. Liz / learn German?
10. Liz / learn French and Spanish?

a. the week
b. the math test last week
c. her classes at the Winfield Language Institute
d. her stay in Bogota last month
e. that terrible movie last Saturday
f. her trip to the U.S. last summer
g. their history class
h. his last flight
i. the night
j. her stay in Germany in 1987

8 Reentry

Prepositions

Complete the following sentences with *in, on, at, during,* or *until*.

1. Ted is going to play soccer ____ Saturday.
2. Liz had to wait ____ the end of the week for an interview.
3. Everybody laughed a lot ____ the movie.
4. Sekila wasn't very happy ____ her first winter in Winfield.
5. ____ 3:30 all the students go home.
6. Toshio is planning to come to Winfield ____ July.
7. Bob is always bored ____ his math class.
8. There's a good movie on TV ____ 9:30.
9. Toshio made a lot of friends ____ his visits to Winfield.
10. It's very hot here ____ August.
11. Last night Gino didn't leave the Roma ____ 11:15.
12. I'm seeing Bob ____ Monday.
13. Joyce was late for school. She didn't get up ____ 8:15.
14. Lisa talks a lot ____ some of her classes.
15. Sekila is never nervous ____ a test.

Presentation

Reporting what someone said

SEKILA:	What did Ms. Roberts say about your résumé?
LIZ:	She **said I had** excellent references.
SEKILA:	What else did she say?
LIZ:	She **said she had to** interview a lot of applicants.

Direct speech	**Indirect speech**
MS. ROBERTS: "You **have** excellent references." $\longrightarrow$	Ms. Roberts said Liz **had** excellent references.
(present tense) $\longrightarrow$	(past tense)

10 **Practice**

Sekila and Liz had coffee after the interview. Report what they said.

SEKILA:	"You look very nervous."
LIZ:	"I'm tired and hungry."

Sekila said Liz looked nervous.
Liz said she was tired and hungry.

1. LIZ: "This coffee is good."
    SEKILA: "I like it, too."
2. LIZ: "There are a lot of applicants for the job."
    SEKILA: "I'm sure there are."
3. LIZ: "I really want to get it."
    SEKILA: "It's a very good job."
4. LIZ: "The personnel manager is a very busy person."
    SEKILA: "Personnel managers are always busy."

5. LIZ: "They're going to call next week."
SEKILA: "That's great."

6. LIZ: "I have to go home soon."
SEKILA: "I have to go back to college."

7. LIZ: "I want to relax at home."
SEKILA: "I have to study until 10:00."

8. LIZ: "It's 5:00."
SEKILA: "It's time to go."

11 Listening

Tim Hartley, Ellen Roberts' assistant, received a lot of telephone calls about the ad for flight attendants. Make three copies of this chart. Listen to three of the telephone calls and complete the notes Tim made about the three callers.

> **Name:** _____ _____
> **Present Occupation:** _____
> **Languages (if any):** _____
> **Time of Interview (if any):** _____

12 Writing

Look at the notes Ms. Roberts took during her interview with Mr. Hatt. Write three paragraphs about his education, work experience, and qualifications.

> **NOTES**
>
> George Hatt
>
> Education:
> - high school graduate
> - attended a secretarial school for one year
> - studied English, Spanish, typing
>
> Work Experience:
> - now working as a bilingual secretary
> - types, writes letters, answers the phone
> - worked as a cashier in a restaurant
>   during summer vacations
>
> Qualifications:
> - speaks two languages well
> - likes to travel
> - very friendly

Before You Read

1. What do you think teachers like a lot about their jobs?
2. What do you think teachers don't like about their jobs?

Useful vocabulary:

1. When you take a **survey**, you ask a lot of people some questions and report the results.
2. **dread** = be very afraid of
3. Your **boss** is the person you work for.

USA Today, an American newspaper, did a survey of 1,174 teachers. Here is part of the newspaper article.

What Teachers Think

(continued from page 2)

More than 60 percent of the teachers surveyed say that it's their students they look forward to most as a new year begins: "curious students," "turned-on students," "students' questions." Dozens responded simply "the kids."

"A new group of students each year refreshes me like the change of seasons," says Ron Becker of Fultondale, Alabama, in his 19th teaching year.

Says Donna Cagle, who teaches elementary school in Niota, Tennessee, "I can hardly wait to show them they *can* learn and will *love* it."

The teachers surveyed have been on the job an average of 18.8 years. Average age: 44. Two-thirds are female, 85 percent are white. Their salaries average about $28,500.

Of every 10, four teach in high school, four in elementary school, two in middle school or junior high.

And they aren't much different from the rest of us when it comes to what they dread most about going back to work. At the top of their list are their bosses.

Comprehension

Read the following statements. Say *True*, *False*, or *I don't know*.

1. The teachers enjoy only the intelligent students.
2. Ron Becker is 19 years old.
3. The teachers in this survey teach in three types of schools.
4. Donna Cagle doesn't like her job very much.
5. The teachers in the survey have a lot of experience.
6. All the teachers in the survey were old.
7. All the teachers in the survey were women.
8. The teachers' main problem is a problem a lot of people have.

Final Activity

A. Working alone, make two copies of the following résumé. First fill in all the
    missing details on *one* of the résumés. Use your imagination and/or real
    information. You could also pretend to be one of the teachers from *13* and
    use information from the reading.

Personal Data

Name: _____

Address: _____

_____

Telephone: _____

Education

19 ____ -19 ____ : _____ (college/graduate school)

19 ____ -19 ____ : _____ (high school)

Work Experience

19 ____ -present: _____

19 ____ -19 ____ : _____

School vacation work: _____

Travel: _____

Languages: _____

Reasons for changing job: _____

B. Now work with a partner. Take turns finding out all the information from each
    other's résumé. Ask questions with *When* and *How long*. Then fill in your
    blank résumé with the information about your partner.

C. Report to the class what you learned about your classmate.

> Monica said she went to high school from 1983 to 1986.

COMMUNICATION
Talking about sports ▪ Describing someone's abilities ▪ Describing how people do things

GRAMMAR
Simple past of irregular verbs: *come, win, lose, beat* ▪ Object pronouns: *me, us, them* ▪ Adverbs: *well, badly, quickly, slowly, beautifully* ▪ *As...as possible*

SKILLS
Reading a newspaper article ▪ Writing a paragraph

They Lost the Game!

Mike and Bob are walking home from school. Bob had a swimming race this afternoon in his gym class.

MIKE: How did your race go?

BOB: Awful! I came in last.

MIKE: Last? You came in first last month. What happened?

BOB: I guess I'm out of shape. Even Gino can beat me. We had a race last night, and he won.

MIKE: Well, you didn't get any exercise for weeks. You just sat home and studied.

BOB: That's true. From now on I'm going to exercise as much as possible.

MIKE: You should go for a long walk every day. That's a really good way to exercise, and doctors say you should walk as quickly as possible.

BOB: Yeah, that's what I'm going to do. Did Ted's team win their soccer match last Saturday?

MIKE: No, they lost three to nothing to Westlake. Ted was really disappointed. Westlake beat them three to nothing the last time, too.

BOB: Let's face it. Ted's not a great soccer player.

MIKE: That's true, but he's a pretty good swimmer.

BOB: I know. I'm not going to have a race with Ted for a month or two!

1 Vocabulary in Context 🔊

Talking about sports

Read the following text. Then find the words and expressions in the text to match the definitions below.

Ted likes swimming and soccer. He's a **pretty good swimmer.** Last week he **won** the 100-meter swimming **race.** Ted and some of his friends are also **on** a soccer **team.** They have a very good **coach.** The coach gives wonderful advice. He thinks his **athletes** need to practice more. He says they should learn to **run fast** and to **kick** the ball very **hard.** Also, the athletes don't stay **calm** enough at soccer **events.** The coach thinks they need to relax more and to **go to bed** early the night before an important **match.**

1. This word means *a group of players.*
2. This person teaches and gives advice to members of a team.
3. This is another word for *a person who plays sports.*
4. You do this when you want to get somewhere very quickly.
5. This is the opposite of *nervous.*
6. You do this with the ball in soccer and football, but not in tennis.

2 Presentation 🔊

Giving sports results; simple past of irregular verbs: *come, win, lose, beat*

A
MIKE:	How was your race?
BOB:	Awful! I **came in** last.
MIKE:	How was Ted's race?
BOB:	Great! He **came in** first.

Some responses:
Great!   Not so good.
Not bad.   Awful!
OK.

B
GINO:	**Did** Ted's team **win** their match last Saturday?
MIKE:	No, they **lost** three to nothing to Westlake.
GINO:	Three to nothing? That's awful!
MIKE:	I know, and Westlake **beat** Winfield three to nothing the last time, too. Well, at least they **won** their match with Riverview.

C
BOB:	**Did** you **win** your soccer match today?
TED:	No, we tied — one to one.

3 Practice

Work with a partner. Take turns asking and answering questions about the results of the races in the chart.

> A: How was Mike's race?
> B: Not so good. He came in ninth.

Name	Result
Mike	ninth
Joyce	third
Tom	tenth
Howard	second
Sekila	first
Gloria	eighth

4 Practice

Work with a partner. Take turns asking and answering questions about the results of the soccer matches in the chart.

> A: Did Winfield win their match on October 19th?
> B: | Yes, they did. They won three to two.
> | Yes, they did. They beat Riverview three to two.
>
> B: Did Riverview win their match on October 19th?
> A: No, they didn't. They lost three to two to Winfield.

Soccer Results				
Teams				Date
Winfield	3	Riverview	2	October 19
Winfield	0	Westlake	3	October 26
Riverview	1	Westlake	2	October 30
Middletown	2	Winfield	3	October 30
Middletown	1	Riverview	0	November 3
Westlake	2	Middletown	1	November 7
Winfield	2	Westlake	2	November 7

Presentation 🔲

Object pronouns: *me, us, them*

A

MIKE:	You came in last! What happened, Bob?
BOB:	I guess I'm out of shape. Even Gino can beat **me**.

I	→	me
we	→	us
they	→	them

B

BOB: Did Winfield beat Riverview in October?
SAM: Yeah, we beat **them** three to two.
BOB: I think they're going to beat **us** next month.
SAM: Oh! Why?
BOB: Because they practice a lot.

6 **Practice**

What would the people say in the following situations? Use: *me, us*, or *them*.

> Ted, before his team's soccer match with Riverview:
>
> "They're good players, but we can beat ___them___ ."

1. Gino, before a swimming race with Sam:
   "He swims very well. He's going to beat ____ ."
2. Gloria and Sekila, before a soccer match on a wet day:
   "We don't have a car, but Sam can take ____ to the match."
3. Toshio, about the Winfield soccer team:
   "They play well. I like to watch ____ ."
4. Ted, after his team's soccer match with Westlake:
   "They're excellent players. They beat ____ ."
5. Elinor, before a tennis match with Howard:
   "I'm out of shape. You're going to beat ____ ."
6. Gloria, before a volleyball game with another school:
   "We have a good team. I think we can beat ____ ."
7. Lisa, to her friend Joyce:
   "I don't know how to swim. Can you teach ____ ?"
8. Gino and Cristina, after the soccer game:
   "We didn't see Sam at the game, but he said that he saw ____ ."

7 **Practice**

Choose the correct pronoun to complete the following sentences.

> Are you going to play Middletown soon, Ted?
> Yes, and we're going to beat ___*them*___ (they/them).

1. Did you play Riverview last month, Ted?
Yes, and (we/us) _____ beat _____ (they/them).
2. Did you play tennis with Joyce today, Lisa?
Yes, I did, and she beat _____ (I/me).
3. Let's go to a movie, Elinor.
Good idea. Why don't you call the Logans and invite
_____ (they/them), too.
4. (I/Me) _____ didn't see Sam or Gino at the soccer match
last Saturday, Ted.
I saw _____ (they/them), but (they/them) _____ left early.
5. (We/Us) _____ would like to learn to play the guitar, Gloria.
Can you teach _____ (we/us)?

8 **Vocabulary in Context**

Describing someone's abilities

runner	BUT	soccer	
swimmer		chess	
skier		volleyball	player
dancer		tennis	
singer		baseball	
ice skater		basketball	

Lisa likes **ice skating.**
She is an excellent **ice skater**.

Sam likes **running**.
He is a very good
runner.

Bob likes **chess**. He is
a good **chess player**.

D

Liz likes **skiing**, but she is only a fair **skier**.

E

Joyce likes **dancing**, but she isn't a very good **dancer**.

F

Gino likes **singing**, but he is a poor **singer**.

9 Interaction

Interview five classmates about their abilities in sports and other recreational activities. Then fill in the chart. Use the vocabulary from *8*. Report what you learn to the class.

A: Do you like ____*skiing*____ ?

B: Yes, | and I'm ____*a good skier*____ .
        | but I'm ____*only a fair skier*____ .

B: No, but I like ____*dancing*____ ,
   and I'm a ____*good dancer*____ .

Name	Activity	Ability

REPORT: Pablo likes dancing, and he's a pretty good dancer.

10 Presentation 📼

Describing how people do things

> Use adverbs to describe how well someone does something.
> **Well, badly, quickly, slowly,** and **beautifully** are adverbs.

A

Cristina likes to play chess, and she plays very **well.**

B

Liz likes to sing, but she **doesn't** sing **very well**.

C

Adela likes to draw, but she draws **badly.**

D

Bob is going to go for a long walk. He is going to walk **quickly.**

E

Howard likes to swim, but he doesn't swim quickly. He swims **slowly**.

F

Lisa likes to sing, and she sings **beautifully.**

11 Practice

Complete the descriptions of the following people by using an adverb from _10_.

1. I think Sekila is going to be famous one day. She sings _____ .
2. No one likes to listen to Gino sing. He sings _____ .
3. Lisa needs to take swimming lessons. She doesn't swim _____ .
4. Howard likes to dance with Elinor. She dances _____ .
5. We saw Ted come in first in the swimming race. He swims _____ .
6. Mike doesn't beat Sam when they play chess. Sam plays _____ .
7. Mike is an excellent runner, and he exercises every day. He runs _____ .
8. Ted is only a fair soccer player. He doesn't play _____ .
9. Adela is a poor tennis player. She plays _____ .
10. Sekila isn't a fast swimmer. She swims _____ .

12 Presentation 🔊

As + as possible

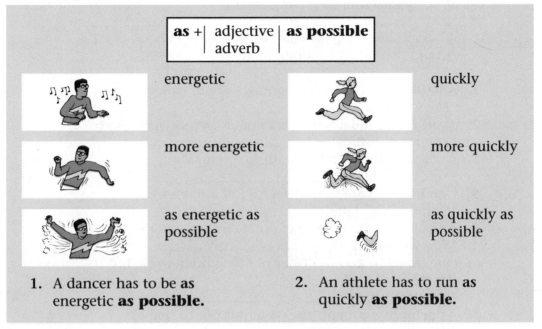

as +	adjective	as possible
	adverb	

energetic

quickly

more energetic

more quickly

as energetic as possible

as quickly as possible

1. A dancer has to be **as** energetic **as possible.**

2. An athlete has to run **as** quickly **as possible.**

13 Practice

Use *as . . . as possible* and one of the following adjectives or adverbs to say what these people have to do or how they have to be: *much, patient, nice, quickly, creative, calm, caring, outgoing, slowly, often.*

> A flight attendant has to be ___*as nice as possible*___ .
> A flight attendant has to help the passengers
> ___*as much as possible*___ .

1. A typist has to type _____ .
2. A teacher has to be _____ .
3. A student has to study _____ .
4. A waiter has to walk _____ .
5. A salesperson has to be _____ .
6. A nurse has to be _____ .
7. During an exam, a student has to think _____ .
8. An artist has to be _____ .
9. A police officer has to be _____ .
10. A soccer player has to practice _____ .

14 Practice

What would the people in the following situations say? Complete their sentences with an expression with *as . . . as possible.*

> A boss to her secretary (she needs a letter very quickly):
> "Could you type this letter ____*as quickly as possible*____ ?"

1. A mother to her son (he's going away to college):
   "Please write _____ ."
2. A father to his daughter (her grades are not very good):
   "You should study _____ ."
3. A coach to his soccer team (before a match):
   "Kick the ball _____ ."
4. One friend to another (before a job interview):
   "Don't forget. Speak _____ ."
5. A coach to an athlete (the athlete isn't playing well):
   "You should practice _____ ."
6. One friend to another (they're doing homework, but they want to go to the movies):
   "Let's finish this _____ ."
7. A doctor to a patient (the patient is out of shape):
   "You should exercise _____ ."
8. Gino to a friend at work (the friend doesn't feel well):
   "You should go home and rest _____ ."

15 Listening

Number your paper from 1-8. Listen to the conversation between Sam and Gino. Then read the statements and write *True, False,* or *I don't know.*

1. Sam's team lost its match.
2. Riverview won the match three to two.
3. Winfield beat Riverview the last time.
4. Sam didn't play very well.
5. Soccer is the only sport Sam plays.
6. Gino is going to practice soccer as often as possible.
7. Gino is out of shape.
8. Gino isn't going to exercise in the winter.

16 Reading

Before You Read

1. What sports do people in your country enjoy most?
2. Who are famous athletes in your country?

> **Useful vocabulary:**
>
> 1. outstanding = very special
> 2. training = an exercise program
> 3. retire = stop working (in this case, stop playing a sport)
> 4. score a goal
>
>

Edson Arantes, known as Pelé, was born in 1940 in Brazil. He was an outstanding soccer player, but as a boy he had no formal training in the sport. He learned to play soccer with his friends on the beaches of Rio de Janeiro. His first match for the Brazilian national soccer team was in 1955, and by 1958 he was a world-famous soccer player. From 1956 to 1968 he scored 1,200 goals for the Santos Club in Brazil and the Brazilian national team. He played for Brazil in four World Cup matches, and Brazil won three of these.

Everybody loved to watch Pelé. He was an excellent athlete and a wonderful team member. He was funny, too. He retired from Brazilian soccer in 1974, and the next year he went to the United States to play for the New York Cosmos. He helped to make the Cosmos team a very good one. He retired from soccer in 1977. He now lives in Brazil where he is a soccer coach.

Comprehension

Complete the chart with information about Pelé.

LAST NAME: _____

FIRST NAME: _____

PLACE OF BIRTH: _____

YEAR OF BIRTH: _____

TRAINING/EXPERIENCE AS A BOY: _____

_____

AGE AT FIRST MATCH FOR THE NATIONAL TEAM: _____

REASONS WHY EVERYONE LOVED TO WATCH HIM:

1. _____ 2. _____ 3. _____

_____ _____ _____

AGE WHEN HE PLAYED FOR BRAZIL FOR THE LAST TIME: _____

NAME OF LAST TEAM HE PLAYED FOR: _____

PRESENT OCCUPATION: _____

17 Writing

Write a paragraph about a famous athlete. Include some or all of the following information.

- Name
- Place of birth
- Date of birth
- When he or she started playing the sport
- Important statistics
- Greatest athletic accomplishment
- Other interesting facts (salary, family, etc.)

18 Reentry

Complete the paragraph with the words on the list.

beat	coach	quickly	nervous	hard
players	soccer	them	they	won

Winfield Wins Soccer Game

Before the (1) _____ match in Middletown, the Winfield team was (2) _____ . Their (3) _____ said, "You played this team last month, and you (4) _____ them. You can beat (5) _____ again."

The Winfield team played well. (6) _____ kicked the ball (7) _____ , and they ran as (8) _____ as possible. The Middletown team had good (9) _____ too, but Winfield (10) _____ the game.

19 Final Activity

Work with a partner. Choose a role, Student A or Student B. Then role play the conversation. You can use some of these questions in your conversation:

Where are you going?
How was . . . ?
What happened . . . ?

STUDENT A: Yesterday you were in a swimming race and you came in first. Now you're going to a friend's house. You meet Student B on the street. You know he or she had a soccer game today. Ask Student B about it.

STUDENT B: You're going home after a soccer match. Your team lost and you played badly. The score was 2-0. You meet Student A on the street. You know Student A was in a swimming race yesterday. Ask him or her about it.

COMMUNICATION
Comparing how people do things ▪
Comparing people and places ▪ Expressing
and explaining wishes and desires ▪ Making
an inference

GRAMMAR
Object pronouns: *him* and *her* ▪
As + adjective/adverb + *as* ▪ *Must be* for
inferences

SKILLS
Reading short biographies ▪ Writing a short
paragraph

I Wish I Could . . .

Toshio is in Winfield again. It's Saturday night, and he's at the Roma with Sam.
Sam just introduced Toshio to Gino. They're talking about sports.

SAM: How's the swimming going, Gino?

GINO: It's OK. I'm improving. One of these days I'm going to be as fast as
          Hajime Ito. Just wait and see!

SAM: Hajime Ito? Who's he? Never heard of him!

GINO: He's a famous Japanese swimmer. I admire him a lot.

SAM: I don't suppose you know him, Toshio?

TOSHIO: As a matter of fact, I do. He's my cousin.

GINO: No kidding! You must be very proud of him.

TOSHIO: Yes, I am. He's a nice guy. I wish I could swim as fast as Hajime,
          but I'm not a very good swimmer.

GINO: What sports do you like?

TOSHIO: I like running. I admire some of the American runners very much.

SAM: Yeah, we have some excellent runners, but my favorite athlete is
          the tennis player Mark Peters. I wish I could go to the next U.S.
          Open in New York to watch him play.

GINO: I like to watch Peters, too, but my favorite tennis player is Larry
          Yang. What do you think of him?

SAM: He's OK, but he isn't as good as Mark Peters.

1 Presentation 📼

Object pronouns: *him* and *her*

A

SAM: Hajime Ito? Who's he?
GINO: He's a famous Japanese swimmer. I admire **him** a lot.

he → him
she → her

B

GINO: Steffi Graf? Who's she?
SAM: She's a famous German tennis player. I admire **her** a lot.

2 Practice

Choose the correct word to complete each sentence.

Gino's idol is Hajime Ito. He admires ___*him*___ (he/him) a lot.

1. Florence Griffith Joyner won three medals at the Olympic Games in Seoul in 1988. Most Americans admire _____ (she/her) very much.
2. Steffi Graf is an outstanding German tennis player. Everyone likes to watch _____ (her/him) play.
3. Toshio's cousin is a nice guy. Toshio likes _____ (her/him) a lot.
4. Bob and Gino had a race at the pool, and Bob is upset because Gino beat _____ (he/him).
5. Joyce doesn't like to play tennis with Ted because Ted always beats _____ (her/him).
6. Cristina is Gino's girlfriend. He loves _____ (she/her) very much.

3 Pronunciation 📼

Repeat these sentences.

1. Hajime Ito? Who's he? Never heard of him!
2. Florence Griffith Joyner? Who's she? Never heard of her!
3. Elvis Presley? Who's he? Never heard of him!
4. Judy Garland? Who's she? Never heard of her!
5. Clint Eastwood? Who's he? Never heard of him!

4 Interaction

Find a partner. Think about what your partner's interests are. Working alone, write the names of three famous people you admire. Choose people you think your partner doesn't know. Then look at your partner's list and find out about the famous people he or she admires.

A: _John Steinbeck_ ? Who's _he_ ?
Never heard of _him_ !
B: _He's a great American writer_ . I admire _him_ a lot.

5 Reentry

Object pronouns: *it, him, her, them*

Complete the paragraph with the appropriate object pronouns.

On Sunday, Toshio is going to write to his grandparents. They are about 75 years old and when Toshio is in Tokyo he likes to visit (1) _____ . They talk to (2) _____ a lot and ask (3) _____ questions about his job. His grandmother was sick a few weeks ago, and the Ito family was very worried about (4) _____ . Fortunately, Toshio's grandfather is a very caring person, and he looked after (5) _____ very well. Toshio's grandfather was a farmer for many years. During their school vacations, Toshio and his sister helped (6) _____ a lot on the farm. Their grandfather was always very kind and patient with (7) _____ . He had a big farm, but he had to sell (8) _____ a few years ago, and he was very sad. Toshio's sister visits their grandparents at least once a week. They love to see (9) _____ , and she loves to see (10) _____ .

6

Presentation 🔲

Comparing how people do things

> Use **as** + *adverb* + **as** to compare how people do things.

1. Ted swims the 100 meters in 1 minute.
   Gino swims the 100 meters in 1 minute.
   Gino swims **as fast as** Ted **does**.
2. Hajime swims very fast.
   Gino swims pretty fast.
   Gino doesn't swim **as fast as** Hajime **does**.
3. I can skate very well.
   Bob can skate pretty well.
   Bob can't skate **as well as** I **can**.
4. I speak Spanish well.
   You speak Spanish very well.
   I don't speak Spanish **as well as** you **do**.

They play tennis as well as	I you we they	do.
	he she	does.

He can speak Spanish as well as	I you he she we they	can.

Practice

Read the following sentences. Then compare how the two people do things. Use words such as: *hard, well, fast, far, early, late, much, beautifully.*

> Adela reads 2 books a month. Elinor reads 2 books a month, too.
> *Adela reads as much as Elinor does.*

> Gloria studies 2 hours a day. Bob studies 3 hours a day.
> *Gloria doesn't study as much as Bob does.*

1. Gino works very hard. Cristina works very hard, too.
2. Lisa ran 5 kilometers yesterday. Joyce ran 5 kilometers, too.

3. Liz walks 10 blocks in 10 minutes. Bob walks 10 blocks in 12 minutes.
4. Gino swam the 100 meters in 1 minute and 15 seconds. Ted swam the 100 meters in 1 minute and 10 seconds.
5. Sam can kick the ball 200 meters. Mike can kick the ball 200 meters.
6. Joyce can type 50 words a minute. Lisa can type 50 words a minute.
7. Gino goes to bed at 1:00 AM. Bob goes to bed at 11:30 PM.
8. Liz can speak a little Spanish. Elinor can speak a little Spanish, too.

8 Interaction

Work with a partner and take turns comparing how two people do things. The people can be famous people or people you know.

A: Gloria plays tennis as well as Liz.

B: That's true.

B: I'm not so sure about that.

9 Presentation

Comparing people and places

A

GINO: What do you think of Larry Yang?

SAM: He's OK, but he isn't **as good as** Mark Peters.

B

TOM: Where would you like to go next summer? Niagara Falls or Lake Placid?

ADELA: It doesn't matter. Niagara Falls is **as beautiful as** Lake Placid.

10 Practice

Work with a partner. Take turns asking and answering questions that compare the following people and places.

---

who / be / Mark Spitz / Adrian Morehouse?
Adrian Morehouse / Mark Spitz / not / fast / Adrian Morehouse
A: Who would you like to be — Mark Spitz or Adrian Morehouse?
B: Adrian Morehouse. Mark Spitz isn't as fast as Adrian Morehouse.

---

who / be / Hajime Ito / Adrian Morehouse?
I don't know / fast
A: Who would you like to be — Hajime Ito or Adrian Morehouse?
B: I don't know. Hajime Ito is as fast as Adrian Morehouse.

1. where / go / Brazil / Costa Rica?
   I don't know / beautiful
2. who / be / Steffi Graf / Gabriela Sabatini?
   Steffi Graf / Gabriela / not / talented / Steffi
3. where / eat dinner / the Roma / the French
   Restaurant?
   I don't know / nice
4. who / listen to / Madonna / Whitney Houston?
   I don't know / good
5. who / meet / Tom Cruise / Dustin Hoffman?
   Dustin Hoffman / Tom Cruise / not /
   interesting / Dustin Hoffman
6. where / live / New York / Anchorage?
   New York / New York / not / cold / Anchorage

11 Interaction

Work with a partner and compare people and places. Tell your partner who you want to and don't want to meet, or where you want to or don't want to go. Use these models to talk about: *famous people, movies, places, and sports teams.*

A: I want to meet Meryl Streep, but I don't want to meet Jane Fonda.
B: Oh, why's that?
A: Because Jane Fonda isn't as interesting as Meryl Streep.

A: I want to go to Washington, but I don't want to go to Miami.
B: Oh, why's that?
A: Because Miami isn't as beautiful as Washington.

---

12 Presentation

Expressing and explaining wishes and desires

A
| GINO: | **Toshio wishes he could** swim as well as Hajime. **I wish I could** swim as well as Hajime, too. |

B
SAM:	**I wish I could** go to the next U.S. Open.
GINO:	Oh, why's that?
SAM:	Because I'd like to watch Mark Peters.

13 Practice

Express the wishes and desires of the people in the pictures.

 Liz wishes she could get a job as a flight attendant.

1.

2.

3.

4.

5.

6.

7.

8.

14 Interaction

Work with a partner. Tell each other about your wishes and desires. Talk about people, places, and possessions.

> A: I wish I could ___buy a guitar___ .
> B: Oh, really? Why's that?
> A: Because ___I would like to learn how to play one___ .

15 Presentation 📼

Making an inference

> Use **must be** to make an inference when you are about 99% sure that what you are saying is a fact.

A
> Toshio: Hajime Ito is my cousin.
> Gino: No kidding! You **must be** very proud of him.

B
> Gino: Hajime Ito won all his races last year.
> Sam: He **must be** an excellent swimmer.

C
> Bob: The soccer team has a big match tomorrow.
> Mike: Really? They **must be** practicing now.

16 Practice

Make inferences about the following situations. Use words such as *busy, happy, nervous, caring, beautiful, cold, worried, in shape, famous, boring, tired* to describe what you think.

> Gino doesn't have time to talk to his friends today.
> He must be very busy.

> The Riverview soccer team is winning all its matches.
> The players must be very happy.

1. Everybody knows that singer.
2. Everybody in Winfield is wearing a coat today.
3. Sekila got a long letter from her family this morning.
4. Adela walked 25 blocks this afternoon.
5. Cristina's mother is very ill in Colombia.
6. Mike Young wins almost all his swimming races.
7. Lisa has a history test today.
8. Brazil has a lot of fantastic beaches.
9. This is a quiet town with only one theater and a few stores.
10. Gloria helps her friends a lot.

17 Listening 📼

Number your paper from 1-5. Listen to each conversation and write the name of the sport the people must be talking about.

> YOU HEAR: "Don't forget, everybody, you should kick the ball as hard as you can."
> WRITE: They must be talking about soccer.

18 Reading

Before You Read

1. Which famous people do you admire?
2. Do many famous people come from your country?
   Who are they?

> **Useful vocabulary:**
>
> 1. **to star in** = to be the most important actor or actress in
> 2. **dynamic** = outgoing
> 3. **shy** = not outgoing
> 4. **modest** = not loud or selfish
> 5. **is close to** = loves very much

Who's Who?

Fred Astaire was born in Omaha, Nebraska in 1899. He was a tap dancer and famous actor, and he starred in many excellent musical films. He was dynamic and extremely hardworking. He liked to wear a top hat when he was dancing. He died in 1987.

James Baldwin, a famous American writer, was born in New York City in 1924. In his books, he wrote about the problems of black Americans and of black people in general. He left the United States in 1948 and went to live in France, where he died in 1987.

Benazir Bhutto became prime minister of Pakistan in 1988 when she was only 35. She studied at Radcliffe College in the United States and at Oxford University in England. She usually wears Pakistani clothes, with a "dupatta," a large scarf, over her head.

Blanche Madonna Louise Ciccone was born in Detroit in 1959. She is a rock singer and a movie star. She has sold millions of copies of some of her records. At her concerts she usually wears unusual clothes.

Albert Einstein was born in Ulm, Germany, in 1879. A great scientist and mathematician, he was a shy, modest man. He liked to live a very simple life, so he didn't cut his hair or wear suits or ties. He became a U.S. citizen in 1940. He died in Princeton, New Jersey, in 1955.

Steffi Graf was born in West Germany in 1970. She is an outstanding, professional tennis player, and in 1988 she won the "Grand Slam," or all four of the major tennis tournaments. Steffi is very close to her family.

Whitney Houston was born in New Jersey in 1964. She is a famous American pop singer. She is tall and beautiful. Her first album sold 14 million copies. She first began to sing as a child in church. She is also very close to her family.

Elvis Presley was born in Memphis, Tennessee, in 1935. He played the guitar, and he was a rock singer and a movie star. Above all, he was for many years the king of rock and roll. He became very rich, but he was generous with his money, and he helped many people. He died in 1977.

Andres Segovia was born in Linares, Spain, in 1893. He began to study the guitar at the age of six, and he gave his first public concert in Granada in 1909. He was an outstanding musician and he played the guitar until he was very old. He died in 1987.

Comprehension

A. Compare the reading texts on page 135 with these photos. Say who you think each person must be.

This must be Elvis Presley because he's playing the guitar and singing.

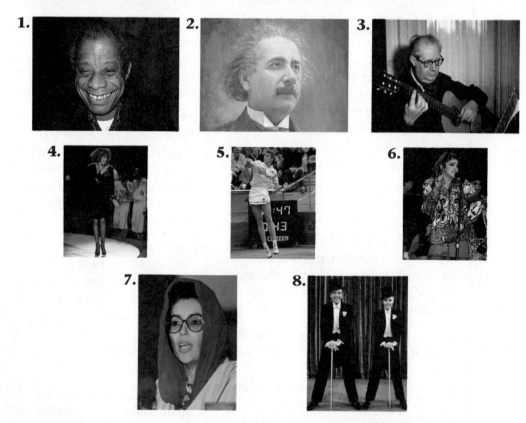

1.

2.

3.

4.

5.

6.

7.

8.

B. Read the texts about the famous people again and complete the following information.

1. Six American citizens are mentioned in the texts. Who are they?

a. _____

b. _____

c. _____

d. _____

e. _____

f. _____

2. Two of the nine people did not die in the country of their birth. Who were they?

a. _____ **b.** _____

3. Andres Segovia and Steffi Graf became famous when they were teenagers. How old was Andres Segovia and how old was Steffi Graf?

a. _____ **b.** _____

4. One of these famous people is the most important person in his or her country. Who is he or she?

_____

19 Writing

Write a short paragraph explaining why you would like to be one of the famous people in *17*. Write another short paragraph explaining why you wouldn't like to be one of the people from *17*.

PARAGRAPH 1: I would like to be _____ because . . .
PARAGRAPH 2: I wouldn't like to be _____ because . . .

20 Final Activity

Talk with a classmate about your wishes and desires. Discuss the following questions. Take notes on your partner's response.

> **Useful vocabulary:**
> The **country** is the opposite of the city.

1. What would you like to be? (For example, pilot, teacher, movie star, etc.) Why?
2. Which famous people do you wish you could meet? Why?
3. Where would you like to live? In Hawaii? In New York City? Why? Where *wouldn't* you like to live? Why?
4. Would you like to live in the country or the city?
5. What do you wish you could buy for your house or apartment? Why?
6. Which countries do you wish you could visit? Why?

When you are finished, tell the class about your partner's wishes and desires.

COMMUNICATION
Identifying body parts and injuries ▪ Talking about accidents and health problems

SKILLS
Reading a news article about an accident ▪ Writing an accident report

GRAMMAR
Who and *what* questions with two-word verbs ▪ Nouns as adjectives ▪ Possessive of plural nouns ▪ Simple past of irregular verbs: *eat, fall, break, hurt, make*

What Happened to Sam?

Adela is at Lisa's school. She's looking for Lisa because Sam had an accident at work. She's talking with Ms. Hill, the school secretary.

MS. HILL: Good morning. May I help you?

ADELA: Good morning. I'm Lisa Logan's mother. Her brother had an accident this morning and . . .

MS. HILL: I'm so sorry to hear that, Mrs. Logan. I hope it isn't serious.

ADELA: I don't think so, but he's in the hospital under observation. I'm going to the hospital now, and I'd like Lisa to come, too.

MS. HILL: Of course, Mrs. Logan. It's lunchtime right now. Let's go look for her in the cafeteria.

GIRL: Who are you looking for?

MS. HILL: Lisa Logan.

GIRL: Oh, yes, I know Lisa. She's in my science class. I saw her here a few minutes ago. Look, she's over there, at the last table.

ADELA: Oh, I see her. Thanks for your help, and thanks to you, too, Ms. Hill.

LISA: Hi, Mom. What are you doing here?

ADELA: Well . . . Sam had an accident this morning and . . .

LISA: Oh, no! What happened?

ADELA: He slipped and fell from a truck. He broke his wrist.

LISA: It isn't too serious, then.

ADELA: No, but he's in the hospital because he hurt his back, too. I'm going to the hospital now, and I want you to come, too.

LISA: Sure, I'll come right away. Could you wait for me over there next to the teachers' room?

1 Presentation 🔲

Who and what questions with two-word verbs

A verb and a preposition can be combined to form a two-word verb. A two-word verb is a verb + a preposition that together have a new meaning.

Talk about is a two-word verb. **Talk about** means *discuss*.

A

GIRL:	**Who** are you **looking for?**
MS. HILL:	Lisa Logan.
GIRL:	Oh, yes, I know Lisa. Look! She's over there.

Two-word verbs:

forget about	talk about
listen to	think about
look at	wait for
look for	worry about
speak to	write to
talk to	

B

ELINOR:	**What** did you and Adela **talk about**?
MIKE:	Sam's accident.

2 Practice

Read the following situations. Use *who* and *what* and the two-word verbs listed in *1* to ask questions.

Gloria visits Sekila. Sekila is writing a letter.
GLORIA: ___*Who are you writing to*___ ?
SEKILA: A friend in Zaire.

1. Cristina comes into the Roma. Gino and Toshio are talking.
   CRISTINA: _____ ?
   GINO: Toshio's cousin, Hajime Ito.

2. You come home. Your sister is listening to the radio.
   YOU: _____ ?
   YOUR SISTER: An opera.

3. Ted comes over to the table where Mike and Bob are looking at pictures.
   TED: _____ ?
   MIKE: Pictures of last Saturday's game.

4. Gloria sees Liz waiting at a table at the Roma.

GLORIA: _____ ?

LIZ: A friend.

5. Howard sees Elinor with a pen and some paper.

HOWARD: _____ ?

ELINOR: My mother.

6. Joyce isn't talking, but she's smiling a lot.

TED: _____ ?

JOYCE: Summer vacation.

7. Mike is looking in the kitchen, in the living room, and in the yard.

ELINOR: _____ ?

MIKE: Ted. I can't find him.

8. Gloria comes into Sekila's apartment. Sekila is talking on the telephone.

GLORIA: _____ ?

SEKILA: My family.

9. Mike sees Gino waiting on the corner of First and Park.

MIKE: _____ ?

GINO: A taxi.

10. Adela looks very worried.

ELINOR: _____ ?

ADELA: Sam. I hope he's going to be OK.

3 Interaction

Work with a partner and take turns asking and answering questions about last weekend's activities. Report what you learn to the class.

A: Who did you talk to last weekend?

B: _____

A: What did you talk about?

B: _____

A: And who did you talk about?

B: _____

Presentation 🔊

Nouns as adjectives

> Remember that nouns can be used as adjectives **before** other nouns. They are always used in the singular.

A

GIRL:	Who are you looking for?
MS. HILL:	Lisa Logan.
GIRL:	Oh, yes, I know Lisa. She's in my **science class.**

B

BOY:	Can I help you?
ADELA:	Yes, thank you. I'm looking for the **school office.**

Practice

Complete the sentences with one of the following words: *train, history, car, Sunday, school, art, opera, soccer, baseball, rock, morning.*

> I catch the _____*school*_____ bus at 8:00 every morning.

1. Adela is too busy to cook very much during the week. She loves to cook _____ dinner because she has more time then.
2. My _____ coach is a nice guy, but he makes me practice kicking the ball a lot.
3. Lisa likes history, and she likes her _____ teacher.
4. That _____ game was very exciting. The score was Detroit 10, New York 9.
5. Elinor is at an _____ class. She is working on a beautiful painting.
6. Maria de los Angeles is a famous _____ singer.
7. We went to a _____ concert last night. My parents didn't like it because the music was too loud.
8. What is your schedule like? Do you have any _____ classes or are they all in the afternoon?
9. Here's the _____ schedule. Look! There's a train at 8:00.
10. Sam wasn't in a _____ accident. He had an accident at work.

6 Practice

Work with a partner. Ask and answer questions about the following people.

> be (past) / Maria Callas
> famous singer / worked in opera
> A: Who was Maria Callas?
> B: She was a famous opera singer.

1. be (past) Elvis Presley
   famous singer / sang rock and roll
2. be (present) / Diego Maradonna
   famous player / plays soccer
3. be (past) / Chris Evert
   outstanding player / played tennis
4. be (past) / Babe Ruth
   famous player / played baseball
5. be (past) / Fred Astaire
   wonderful dancer / danced tap
6. be (present) / Whitney Houston and Billy Joel
   American singers / sing pop
7. be (present) / Maria de los Angeles
   outstanding singer / sings opera
8. be (past) / Mickey Mantle and Lou Gehrig
   famous players / played baseball
9. be (present) / Kate Warren
   excellent teacher / teaches history
10. be (present) / George Sims
    excellent coach / teaches soccer

7 Presentation

Possessive of plural nouns

> Add an apostrophe after the **s** of regular plural nouns.
> Add an apostophe and then **s** to irregular plurals.

A

LISA: Wait for me over there, next to the **teachers'** room.
ADELA: OK.

B

MS. HILL: What are your **children's** names?
MOTHER: Rebecca and Robert.

8 Practice

Read the sentences below and decide if the words in dark type require an apostrophe before the s, after the s, or if they do not require an apostrophe.

> The **teachers** room is on the first floor.
>
> The **teachers'** room is on the first floor.

> The **nurses** have lunch at 12:00.
>
> The **nurses** have lunch at 12:00.

1. The **Youngs** have a house on South Kennedy Avenue.
2. The **Yankees** coach is fantastic.
3. The **childrens** park is open from 10:00 to 4:00.
4. The **athletes** eat a lot of good food.
5. The **boys** bedrooms are on the second floor.
6. The **girls** mothers come for them in the afternoon.
7. The **mens** coats are on the second floor.
8. That **womens** magazine is excellent.
9. The **Logans** have an old car.
10. The **flight attendants** training program is long.
11. The **Navas** trip to America was a lot of fun.
12. My **sisters** like living in Miami.

9 Practice

Copy the paragraph. Add an apostrophe where necessary.

> Bobs soccer coach is worried about him at the moment.
> **Bob's** soccer coach is worried about him at the moment.

Bobs soccer coach is worried about him at the moment. He says he should get more exercise, but Bobs parents say he should study more. Bob wants to take his parents advice, and he wants to take his coachs advice, too, but it isn't easy. Last night he talked to Gino and Ted, and they said he should get more exercise, but Bob knows that his friends advice is not always good. The Logans are interested in their childrens school and sport activities, but they think Bobs love of sports is too great. There's a parents night at the high school next week, and Tom Logan is going to talk to his sons teachers about his sons progress. The Logans think their sons teachers advice is very important.

10 Vocabulary in Context 🔊

Identifying body parts and injuries

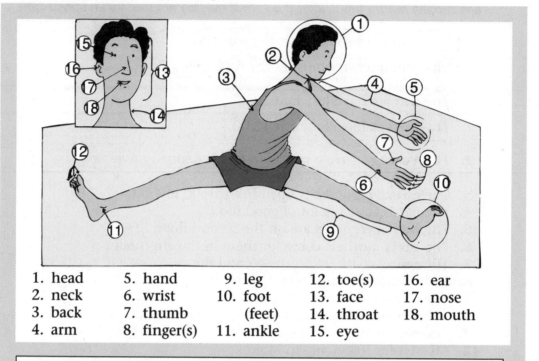

1. head	5. hand	9. leg	12. toe(s)	16. ear
2. neck	6. wrist	10. foot	13. face	17. nose
3. back	7. thumb	(feet)	14. throat	18. mouth
4. arm	8. finger(s)	11. ankle	15. eye	

> With parts of the body, use possessive adjectives: Sam broke **his** wrist.
> Use **break** for bones; use **hurt** for pains that are strong.'
> Use **ache** for pains that are not so strong, but usually last a long time.

1. Be careful! You can break your wrist.
2. Sam's head hurts.
3. His back aches, too.

Useful expressions:

have a | stomachache
          | headache
          | earache
          | backache

11 Practice

Say which parts of the body listed in *10* we can break in an accident.

> We can break our legs.

12 Practice

Describe the problems people in certain occupations have with parts of the body. Use the verb *ache*.

> After a busy day, a typist's ___*back and fingers ache.*___ .

1. After a noisy class, a teacher's _____ .
2. After a busy day, a waitress's _____ .
3. After a race, a runner's _____ .
4. After work, a nurse's _____ .
5. After a game, a coach's _____ .
6. After a concert, a singer's _____ .
7. After a long day, a writer's _____ .
8. After a busy day, a computer programmer's _____ .

13 Listening

Number your paper from 1-10. Listen to some incomplete sentences. Write the part of the body that completes each sentence.

> YOU HEAR: We know a person because we remember his or her _____ .
> WRITE: face

14 Presentation

Talking about accidents and health problems

ADELA: Sam had an accident at work this morning.
LISA: Oh, no! **What happened**?
ADELA: He **fell** from a truck and **broke** his wrist.

ELINOR: Joyce stayed home from school today.
HOWARD: Oh? **What's the matter with her**?
ELINOR: She **ate** too much last night and her stomach **hurt** during the night.

C

MS. HILL: You don't look very well. **What's the matter**, Ms. Warren?
MS. WARREN: My class **made** a lot of noise during the last class and my head aches.

15 Practice

Ask and answer questions about the problems of the people in the pictures.

A: Pablo had an accident.
B: Oh, no! What happened?
A: He fell from a tree and broke his arm.

A: Sekila isn't feeling well.
B: Oh? What's the matter?
A: She went to a party last night and her head hurts.

1.

4.

2.

5.

3.

6.

16 Interaction

Work with a partner. Take turns telling about real or imaginary accidents.

> A: _____ had an accident.
> B: Oh, no! What happened?
> A: Well, | he | _____ .
> | she |

17 Reading

Before You Read

1. What kind of accidents are reported in the newspaper?
2. What information is reported in newspaper articles about accidents?

Useful vocabulary:

1. **deputy** = police officer
2. **avoid** = move away from
3. **lose control**

4. **ditch**

Accident Leaves Two Injured

1 TAWAS CITY—Two men were slightly injured in an automobile
2 accident Saturday evening in the Sherman Township.

3 Joseph Kennedy, 37, of Toledo, Ohio, told Losco County
4 Sheriff's Department deputies that he was driving along National
5 City Road near Turtle Road when he saw an oncoming car
6 cross the center line and enter his lane.

7 Kennedy avoided the oncoming car, but lost control and rolled
8 his auto into a roadside ditch. Riding with Kennedy were Paul
9 Newton, 31, of Adrian, and Cynthia Moore, 46, of Turner.
10 Newton also received minor injuries while Moore was unhurt.

Comprehension

A. Find the word from the reading.

1. In Line 1, it means the opposite of **seriously**.
2. In Line 1, it means the same as **hurt**.
3. In Line 1, it means the same as **car**.
4. In Line 5, it means the same as **coming from the opposite direction**.
5. In Line 6, it means the same as **part of a road**.
6. In Line 8, it is the short form of **automobile**.
7. In Line 10, it means the same as **not very serious**.
8. In Line 10, it means the opposite of **hurt**.

B. Complete the information.

1. Report sent to the newspaper from: _____
2. Kind of accident: _____
3. Time of day accident happened: _____
4. Name of driver: _____
5. Address of driver: _____
6. Exact place of accident: _____
7. Number of cars in accident: _____
8. Number of people in Kennedy's car: _____
9. Names of people hurt: _____
10. Name of person unhurt: _____

18 Writing

Use the information from the following accident report to write a complete paragraph about an accident.

Date of accident: November 11

Time of accident: 4:30 PM

Place of accident: Winfield Park

Name of person or people in accident: Jack Marshall

Description of accident: fell from tree

Injuries: broke leg

Brought to Winfield Hospital by: Bob Logan and Mike Young

19 Reentry

Complete the paragraph with the simple past tense of one of these verbs: *have to, be, lose, hurt, break, have, say.* You can use some verbs more than once.

Last week Cristina's family in Colombia (1) _____ very unhappy

because a member of the family, Ernesto Silva, (2) _____ an

accident. He (3) _____ a passenger in a friend's car and the driver

(4) _____ control. The car hit a large tree and the driver and his

three passengers (5) _____ hurt. They (6) _____ go to

a hospital in Bogota. Ernesto (7) _____ his arm and

(8) _____ his head badly. The doctors (9) _____ that

Ernesto (10) _____ stay in the hospital for a week.

20 Final Activity

Did you ever break or hurt a part of your body? An arm or leg? Did you ever stay in a hospital? Talk with your partner about what happened. Here is a model.

> A: I broke my ankle.
>
> B: Oh really? When did you break it?
>
> A: In 1989.
>
> B: What happened?
>
> A: I fell on the ice in front of my house.
>
> B: Did you go to the hospital?
>
> A: Yes, I did. But I didn't have to stay there.

UNIT 14

COMMUNICATION
Expressing admiration and disappointment ▪ Describing a person's personality ▪ Making comparisons

GRAMMAR
What a + (adjective) + noun ▪ Time expressions with *the...before ...* ▪ *Both* with nouns and pronouns ▪ Comparatives ▪ Irregular comparative forms: *good* and *bad* ▪

SKILLS
Reading a letter ▪ Writing a letter

What a Day!

Gino and Cristina have a date tonight. Gino is waiting for Cristina, but she's late. Finally she arrives.

CRISTINA: Hi, Gino!

GINO: Hi, Cristina! Look at the time! You're more than an hour late!

CRISTINA: And what happened the week before last? You were two hours late for a date.

GINO: Yeah, but I had a problem at the Roma.

CRISTINA: Sure, and I don't have any problems! I work a shorter day than you and have longer vacations, so I don't have any problems! Right?

GINO: Don't be unreasonable, Cristina! You know I don't think that.

CRISTINA: Oh, yes, you do! And you think you work harder than I do, too.

GINO: Listen, Cristina, we're both tired and upset, so why don't we forget this silly fight and go and eat dinner.

CRISTINA: OK . . . OK . . . where do you want to go?

GINO: How about the French restaurant?

CRISTINA: It's too expensive. Why don't we go to the Chinese restaurant?

GINO: The food is better at the French restaurant, Cristina. Let's go there tonight! And don't worry about the money. It's on me.

CRISTINA: OK, let's go! . . . Oh no! Look! It's raining again. The weather is worse than it was yesterday. What a day!

1 Presentation

Expressing admiration and disappointment

> 1. Cristina had a lot of problems today.
>   She says, "What an awful day!"
> 2. Elinor likes a painting very much.
>   She says, "What a beautiful painting!"

2 Pronunciation

Repeat these sentences with the same stress and intonation.

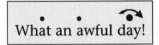

1. What a wonderful life!
2. What an awful year!
3. What an interesting job!

4. What a busy week!
5. What a terrible problem!

3 Practice

What do you say in the following situations? Use these adjectives (or others) to express admiration or disappointment: *wonderful, boring, terrible, fantastic, delicious, awful, exciting, great.*

> It's cold, wet, and windy. You pass your friend on the street.
>
> "What an awful day!"

1. You and a friend are leaving the theater. You hated the movie.
2. You are visiting Dover, a very small and quiet town.
3. You are driving in the country, and you see a bad car accident.
4. You and your sister are watching a soccer match. The score is 4 to 3.
5. You are returning home after seeing Luciano Pavarotti, the opera singer, in concert.
6. You are having a great time at Mary's party. You see Mary.
7. You and a friend at work don't like your boss because she says you have to work every weekend.
8. You are eating at your friend's house. You love the food.

Presentation 🖭

Time expressions with *the . . . before . . .*

1. It's Sunday night. **The night before last** was Friday night.
2. It's my third week at work. **The week before last** was my first week.
3. It's May. **The month before last** was March.
4. It's 1990. **The year before last** was 1988.
BUT:
5. It's Monday. **The day before yesterday** was Saturday.

---

5 **Practice**

Complete the sentences with a time expression.

| Today is Friday. The ___*day before yesterday*___ was Wednesday. |

1. It's 1991. The _____ was 1989.
2. Last week I was busy. The _____ I wasn't.
3. It's April. The _____ was February.
4. It's Monday night. The _____ was Saturday night.
5. It was sunny last week. The _____ it was very wet.
6. It's September. The _____ was July.
7. It's 1992. 1990 was the _____ .
8. It's Thursday . The _____ was Tuesday.
9. It rained last night. The _____ it rained, too.
10. It's my third day at school. The _____ was my first day.

---

6 **Interaction**

Work with a partner to find out about his or her activities in the past.

| A: What did you do the _____ before _____ . |
| B: I _____ . And what did you do? |
| A: I _____ . And what did you do the |
| _____ before _____ ? |
| B: I _____ . |

Both with nouns

> **Both** emphasizes the fact that two people or two things have something in common.

1. **Both** Cristina and Gino were upset.
2. **Both** biology and history are interesting subjects.

8 **Practice**

Say what the people and things in the following pictures have in common.

Both Liz and Gino like to go for long walks.

9 Practice

Look again at page 135 and make 6 sentences with *both* to emphasize what these pairs of famous people have in common. Use the present or past tense, as appropriate.

> Segovia / Presley
> Both Segovia and Presley played the guitar.

1. Madonna / Houston   **3.** Presley / Astaire   **5.** Segovia / Astaire
2. Graf / Einstein   **4.** Houston / Graf

10 Presentation

Both with pronouns

1. In a sentence with a pronoun, **both** comes after *am, is, are, was,* or *were.*
   We're **both** upset.
2. **Both** also comes after auxiliary verbs like *can* or *should.*
   You should **both** study.
3. **Both** comes before other verbs.
   They **both** like Elvis Presley.

Tom:	Who wants to go to the movies? Sam or Bob?
Adela:	They **both** want to go to the movies.

Sekila:	Who can play soccer well? Mike or Ted?
Gloria:	They can **both** play well.

11 Practice

Work with a partner. Ask and answer questions about the people in the chart below. Be sure to use the correct verb.

> A: Who's funny? Ted or Bob?
> B: They're both funny.

> A: Who can play tennis well? Joyce or Gloria?
> B: They can both play tennis well.

> A: Who likes to paint? Gino or Bob?
> B: They both like to paint.

Name	Sports	Pastimes	Languages	Personality
Bob	plays soccer well	paints	Spanish	modest; funny
Ted	swims well	plays chess	French	funny; caring
Joyce	plays tennis well	reads	French	patient
Gino	swims well	paints; reads	Italian	patient
Lisa	plays soccer well	sews; plays chess	Italian	modest
Gloria	plays tennis well	sews	Spanish	caring

12 Interaction

Work with a partner. Take turns asking and answering questions about people or places in your class, town, or country. Say what they have in common.

> A: What do you know about   *Mr. Beatty and Ms. Warren*   ?
> B: Well, they both   _*teach math*_   .

> A: What do you know about   *Rio de Janeiro and São Paolo*   ?
> B: Well, they're both   _*in Brazil*_   .

13 Vocabulary in Context

Describing a person's personality

1   Both Gino and Cristina are **hardworking**; they are not **lazy**. They
2 are going to get married, so they are both trying to save money to buy
3 an apartment. Cristina is usually a very **considerate** person. She
4 knows Gino works very hard so she helps him a lot. She understands
5 why they cannot spend a lot of money on the movies or on meals in
6 restaurants. But, sometimes Gino is **inconsiderate**. He arrives late for
7 his dates with Cristina, and sometimes he forgets about them. But Gino
8 is usually very **reasonable**. He knows he is **unreasonable** at times
9 and he apologizes. Cristina can be a little **unforgiving**. Sometimes
10 she doesn't accept Gino's apologies immediately; she waits for a few
11 days before she speaks to him again. After a fight Gino tries to be
12 considerate and then Cristina is more **forgiving**. Fortunately, both
13 Cristina and Gino are **unselfish**. They aren't **selfish** with their time
14 and money. When Gino has some extra time or money, he shares it
15 with Cristina, and Cristina shares her extra time and money with Gino.

14 Practice

A.   Complete the following sentences with words from *13*.

1. **Lazy** (Line 1) is the opposite of _____ .

2. **Considerate** (Line 3) is the opposite of _____ .

3. **Reasonable** (Line 8) is the opposite of _____ .

4. **Unforgiving** (Line 9) is the opposite of _____ .

5. **Unselfish** (Line 13) is the opposite of _____ .

B.   Both Cristina and Gino have negative and positive personality traits. Read the text again and complete this chart.

Cristina's Personality	Gino's Personality

1. Negative: _____
 2. Positive: **a.** _____
            b. _____
            c. _____
	1. Negative: _____
	 2. Positive: **a.** _____
	            b. _____
	            c. _____

15 Listening

Number your paper from 1-8. Listen and complete the sentences with an adjective that describes the *Intercom 2000* characters. Use the new words you learned in *13* and other words such as *caring* or *patient*.

> YOU HEAR: Tom and Adela are in the kitchen. Tom says, "You look very tired, honey. Go and relax. I can cook dinner."
> YOU WRITE: Tom is ___*considerate*___ .

1. Sam is _____ .

2. Lisa is _____ .

3. Joyce is _____ .

4. Lisa is _____ .

5. Howard is _____ .

6. Sekila is _____ .

7. Gloria is _____ .

8. Elinor is _____ .

16 Presentation

Making comparisons

> To form the comparative, add **-er** to one-syllable adjectives and adverbs.
>   short   +   **-er**   =   shorter
>   fast   +   **-er**   =   faster
> Add **-r** if the adjective or adverb ends in **e**.
>   nice   +   **-r**   =   nicer
> **Than** links the two people or things you are comparing.

> CRISTINA: I work a **shorter** day and have **longer** vacations, so I don't have any problems! Right?
> GINO: Don't be unreasonable, Cristina. You know I don't think that.
> CRISTINA: And you think you work **harder than** I do.
> GINO: No, I don't. Come on! Let's forget this silly fight.

17 Practice

Combine the information in each pair of sentences. Use the comparative form of the following adjectives or adverbs: *warm, cold, deep, hard, fast, nice, long, small, old.*

> Gino's working day is 9 hours. Cristina's working day is 8 hours.
> Gino's working day is longer than Cristina's.

1. Gino's vacation is for two weeks. Cristina's vacation is for three weeks.

2. Howard works six days a week. Tom works five days a week.

3. Mike is 17. Bob is 16.

4. The Nile River is 4,155 miles long. The Amazon River is 4,007 miles long.

5. The Pacific Ocean is 36,409 feet deep. The Atlantic Ocean is 28,538 feet deep.

6. Sekila ran the 100 meters in 12.5 seconds. Gloria ran the 100 meters in 13.5 seconds.

7. It's 72°F in Mexico City today. It's 70°F in San Juan, Puerto Rico.

8. It was 28°F in New York City yesterday. It was 30°F in Winfield.

9. Rhode Island is 1,214 square miles. Connecticut is 5,009 square miles.

10. Liz says dogs are very nice pets. She says cats are nice pets.

18 Practice

Work in small groups. Each group writes five sentences comparing a person in your class with two other people, or a place in your town or country with two other places. (Write about five different people or places.) Use words such as: *small, tall, warm, cold, high, deep, long, cool, nice, short, fast, hard.*

Read your sentences to the class, but do not use the names of the person or place. The class has to guess who or where it is.

> This town is colder than Atlanta, but warmer than Anchorage.

19 Presentation

Irregular comparative forms: *good* and *bad*

CRISTINA: Let's go to the Chinese restaurant.
GINO: Why don't we go to the French restaurant? They have **better** food than the Chinese restaurant.
CRISTINA: OK . . . Oh no! Look! It's raining again. The weather today is **worse** than yesterday. What a day!

20 Practice

Use *better* or *worse* to compare the following people, places, or things.

Cristina had a good day yesterday. She didn't have a very good day today.

Cristina had a better day yesterday than today.

The weather was bad yesterday. The weather is very bad today.

The weather today is worse than yesterday.

1. Cristina is a good cook. Gino is an excellent cook.
2. Winters are bad in Chicago. They are very bad in Anchorage.
3. Gino had a bad day yesterday. He had a very bad day today.
4. Ted saw an exciting movie on Saturday. He saw a very exciting movie on Sunday.
5. Adela's a terrible skater. Elinor's a bad skater.
6. Toshio's a fair cook. Gloria's a poor cook.
7. Liz is a bad singer. Sam is a terrible singer.
8. Ted is an excellent swimmer. Gino's a good swimmer.
9. Bob's a very fast typist. Sekila's a pretty good typist.
10. Sam's a wonderful soccer player. Gino's a good soccer player.

21 Interaction

Work with a partner. Use the comparative of adjectives and adverbs to give reasons for your preferences in *places to visit, restaurants to eat at, records to buy, people to invite to a party.*

> A: Let's ___go to Nelson's coffee shop___ .
> B: No, let's ___go to the Roma___ .
> A: Why do you want to ___go to the Roma___ ?
> B: Because ___the food is better___ .

22 Reading

Before You Read

1. Some people write to magazines or newspapers about their problems. Do you think this is a good idea? Why or why not?
2. What is the name of the section for this kind of letter in a newspaper or magazine you know?

> **Useful vocabulary:**
>
> 1. **teenage** = between 13 and 19 years old
> 2. **take seriously** = think something is important

> **M**y two teenage children are making my life miserable. I love them very much, but they are selfish and lazy. They don't take their schoolwork seriously. I am 40, and life is too short to live like this. What can I do?

Comprehension

A. Now complete the missing information about the following topics.

INFORMATION ABOUT THE WRITER: **1.** _____
2. _____

PROBLEMS: **1.** _____
2. _____
3. _____

B. What would you say to the writer of this letter? Write your answer. Then share it with your classmates.

23 Writing

The sentences below are from two letters to an advice column. Both contain the following information: information about the writer, a description of the problem, and a solution. Read the sentences and try to find which sentences came from which letter. On a piece of paper, write the numbers of all the sentences that you think belong to Letter 1 (in the correct order) and the ones you think belong to Letter 2. When you are sure you have found both letters, write them out.

1. We don't have any children, but we have a nice home and a lot of money.
2. We love them very much, and they love us.
3. We are thinking of leaving home. Is this the right solution?
4. My wife is a business person, too.
5. We are very close and we have wonderful parents.
6. I am a 50-year-old businessman.
7. Unfortunately, they don't like our friends, so we can't see them very often.
8. However, we are both a bit bored with our lives.
9. They say our friends are lazy, inconsiderate, and very selfish.
10. We would like to adopt a couple of kids. Is this a good idea?
11. My brother and I are teenagers.
12. We are really upset because we love our friends, too, and we want to spend a lot of time with them.

24 Final Activity

Compare your life with a classmate's life. Ask him or her these questions and four more of your own.

1. How old are you?
2. How many people are there in your family?
3. What time do you go to bed?
4. What time do you get up?
5. How many hours a day do you work?
6. How long are your vacations every year?

Now, tell the class what you found out about your classmate.

> Sonia is younger than I am. She is 16 and I am 17. We both have three people in our families. She goes to bed earlier than I do . . .

COMMUNICATION
Talking about a continuing condition

GRAMMAR
Contrast between *come* and *go* ▪ *If* clauses
in present tense ▪ Adverb *still* ▪ *And so* +
be or modal auxiliaries ▪ *And so* + *do/does/did* .

SKILLS
Listening to a news bulletin ▪ Reading a
health brochure ▪ Writing health advice

How Are You Feeling?

Gloria and Sekila came to visit Sam at the hospital.

GLORIA: Hi, Sam. How are you doing?
SEKILA: Hello, Sam. I hope you're
feeling better.

SAM: Hi, Sekila. Hi, Gloria. Nice of
you to come.
SEKILA: How are you feeling, Sam?
What do the doctors say?

SAM: Oh, I'm a little better . . . but not much. My back aches and if I
move my head quickly, it really hurts.
SEKILA: Sorry to hear that, Sam. But what do the doctors say?
SAM: They're waiting for the results of some tests. If they're OK, I can go
home at the end of the week.
GLORIA: That's great! Hey, do you want to hear all the Winfield gossip?
SAM: Sure!
GLORIA: Well, Cristina and Gino had a fight.
SAM: So what else is new? Come on! Tell me something interesting.
GLORIA: Well, Liz Young's looking for a new job.
SAM: Liz? Looking for a new job? Now that really is news!
SEKILA: Gino is coming to see you tonight, and so are Mr. and Mrs. Young.
SAM: Great! Gino can tell me all the soccer news.
SEKILA: The Chinese art exhibit is still at the Art Museum. They say it's
excellent.
SAM: I'd like to see it. Maybe we can all go next week.
SEKILA: That's a good idea. It will be there until the end of the month.

Presentation

Contrast between *come* and *go*

> Use **come** when the movement is toward the direction of the speaker or listener.
> Use **go** when the movement is away from the speaker or listener.

A

SEKILA: Gino is **coming** to see you tonight.

B

SEKILA: The Chinese art exhibit is still at the Art Museum.
SAM: I'd like to see that. Maybe we can all **go** next week.

2 **Practice**

Last night the Logans went to the Youngs' for dinner. Complete the sentences about their visit with *come* or *go*.

1. "Please ____ in," Howard said as he opened the door.
2. After dinner Elinor said, "Let's ____ for a walk."
3. Mike had to study so he didn't ____ with them.
4. Joyce stayed at home, too, because she had to ____ to bed early.
5. Elinor asked about Toshio, and Adela said, "He's ____ to Winfield again very soon."

Practice

Complete the following conversations with the correct tense and form of *come* or *go.*

1. ADELA: There's a good movie at the York Theater tomorrow night.
   ELINOR: Why don't we _____ ?
   ADELA: That's a good idea.
2. GINO: How are you feeling today?
   SAM: Much better, thank you.
   GINO: Maria is _____ to see you tonight.
   SAM: Great! That's very nice of her.
3. ANA: What did you do last Sunday?
   SEKILA: I _____ to see a friend in the hospital.
4. JOYCE: Hi, Lisa. Did you hear the news?
   LISA: No. What?
   JOYCE: Whitney Houston is _____ to Winfield!
   LISA: That's wonderful news! Let's _____ to her concert.
   JOYCE: Great idea! And let's _____ to Billy Joel's concert next month, too!

4 **Interaction**

Move around the room. Talk to at least five other students. Take turns extending and refusing invitations with *come* and *go.* Use words like: *lunch, dinner, a barbecue, dessert, coffee, a party.* Here is a model.

> A: Can you come to my place for lunch next Friday?
> B: Thanks a lot, but I can't. I'm going to the dentist.

5 **Presentation**

If **clauses in present tense**

A SAM: If I move my head quickly, it hurts.

B ELINOR: If I need some exercise, I go for a walk.

C
> Gino: If the weather is good, my family goes to the beach.

D
> Howard: What do you do if you can't sleep at night?
> Tom: If I can't sleep, I drink a glass of warm milk.

6 Practice

Use *if* to combine the actions on the left with the ones on the right.

> **1 + e** If Gino is busy at the Roma, he is usually late for his date with Cristina.

1. If Gino is busy at the Roma,
2. If Tom can't sleep at night,
3. If I have a headache,
4. If Sekila gets a cold,
5. If the weather is very cold,
6. If Adela feels very tired,
7. If Toshio is busy during a flight,
8. If Cristina has a problem at work,
9. If Sekila doesn't get a letter from her family,
10. If Joyce reads a lot,

a. Gloria wears a lot of warm clothes.
b. she worries.
c. she goes to bed early.
d. I take an aspirin.
e. he is usually late for his date with Cristina.
f. her eyes hurt.
g. he has a glass of warm milk.
h. she drinks a lot of orange juice.
i. his legs hurt the next day.
j. she tells Gino about it.

7 Practice

Complete the sentences with information about what you do in these situations.

1. If I have time on the weekend, ——————— .
2. If I have a lot of homework, ——————— .
3. If I have a serious problem, ——————— .
4. If the weather is awful, ——————— .
5. If my parents are sick, ——————— .
6. If I'm hungry late at night, ——————— .
7. If I don't feel well, ——————— .
8. If I get up late in the morning, ——————— .
9. If I get to school or work early, ——————— .
10. If I don't get a letter from my family/friend, ——————— .

8 Interaction

Work with a partner and use the information in your sentences in 7. Take turns asking and telling about what you do in these situations.

A: What do you do if _____ ?
B: I _____ . And what do you do?
A: I _____ .

9 Reentry

Simple past tense of regular and irregular verbs

Complete the paragraph with the simple past tense of the following verbs: *ask, want, ache, visit, go, be, say, have, hurt, tell.*

Gloria and Sekila (1) _____ to visit Sam in the hospital. Sam said he (2) _____ OK, but his back (3) _____ , and his head (4) _____ if he moved it quickly. Gloria (5) _____ Sam about Cristina's fight with Gino but Sam didn't take it seriously. He (6) _____ , "Cristina and Gino fight at least once a week." There's a Chinese art exhibit at the Art Museum. Sekila's friends (7) _____ to see it. They (8) _____ it was excellent. Sam (9) _____ Sekila about the exhibit. Sam is going to see it when he leaves the hospital. Gino also (10) _____ Sam, and he (11) _____ him all the soccer news.

10 Presentation 📼

Talking about a continuing condition

> Use **still** to talk about something that was true in the past and is true now.

1. **Still** usually comes between the subject and the verb.
    Sam's head **still** hurts.
    Does his back **still** ache?
    He **still** can't leave the hospital.
    He **still** isn't home.

2. **Still** comes after the verb *be* in affirmative sentences.
    He's **still** in the hospital.
    They are **still** waiting for the test results.

11 Practice

Add *still* to the following sentences. Be sure to put it in the appropriate place.

> Sam is in the hospital.
>
> Sam is still in the hospital.

1. Sam doesn't feel much better.
2. The doctors are unhappy about Sam.
3. Sam can't understand how the accident happened.
4. In the hospital Gino asked Sam, "Do you want to hear all the soccer news?"
5. "Of course, I want to," said Sam.
6. Gloria told Sam, "Cristina is mad at Gino."
7. The Chinese art exhibit is at the Art Museum.
8. Sam wants to go to see it.
9. Adela is worried about Sam.
10. She asked the doctor, "Why does his head hurt?"
11. The doctors don't know the results of the tests.
12. Sam can't leave the hospital.

12 Practice

A. **Think about your life five years ago. Write five sentences about things in your life that are still the same today. Use *still*.**

> I still live with my parents.
> Bruce Springsteen is still my favorite singer.

B. **Read a classmate's sentences and tell the class what you learn about him or her.**

> Meryl Streep is still Tiko's favorite actress. Tiko still lives in a small apartment. He still can't cook very well. His parents still live in Japan. He still plays baseball every Saturday.

13 Listening

A. *First Listening.* **Number your paper from 1-12. Listen to the radio news bulletin the first time. Then complete the information for 1-5.**

1. This is the 8:00 news for February _____ .
2. News Item One is about a department store and a _____ .
3. News Item Two is about a/an _____ .
4. News Item Three is about a _____ .
5. News Item Four is about the _____ .

B. *Second Listening.* **Listen to the news bulletin again. Now complete the information for 6-12.**

6. Location of the new department store: _____
7. Location of the new hotel: _____
8. Place of the accident: _____
9. Number of people in the hospital as a result of the accident: ____
10. Results of the basketball game: _____
11. Temperature in Winfield today: _____
12. Tomorrow's weather: _____

14 Presentation

And so + be or modal auxiliaries

1. Adela is worried. Tom is worried.
   Adela is worried, **and so is** Tom.

2. Gloria can go to the exhibit.
   Sekila can go to the exhibit.
   Gloria can go to the exhibit, **and so can** Sekila.

3. Sam should study.
   Bob should study.
   Sam should study, **and so should** Bob.

15 Practice

Combine the following information with *and so*.

> Lisa / is a high school student / Joyce
>
> Lisa is a high school student, and so is Joyce.

1. Adela / should relax more / Liz
2. Sam / was tired last night / Gino
3. Ted / should work more / Lisa
4. Sekila / can run fast / Mike
5. Tom / was happy yesterday / Adela
6. Costa Rica / is a beautiful country / Brazil
7. Tom / is working in the yard / Elinor
8. I / can do this exercise / you
9. Winfield / is a pretty town / Riverside
10. Gino / can cook well / Cristina

16 Presentation

And so + do/does/did

A

Sam's head hurts. Sam's neck hurts.
Sam's head hurts, **and so does** his
neck.

B

The Logans have a car. The Youngs
have a car.
The Logans have a car, **and so do**
the Youngs.

C

Gloria visited Sam. Sekila visited Sam.
Gloria visited Sam, **and so did** Sekila.

Practice

Combine the information on the left with the appropriate information on the right.
Use *and so* + *do*, *does*, or *did* in your sentences.

> **1 + i** Sam plays soccer, and so does Mike.

1. Sam plays soccer.
2. Adela walks to work.
3. Melanie went on vacation.
4. Sekila works hard.
5. Ted and Bob like comedies.
6. Howard went to a football game.
7. The Navas read a lot.
8. Steffi played well.
9. My friend plays the guitar.
10. Elinor listened to the opera.

a. Elinor and Adela like comedies.
b. Howard listened to the opera.
c. Martina played well.
d. Joyce went to a football game.
e. The Youngs read a lot.
f. I play the guitar.
g. Liz walks to work.
h. Gloria works hard.
i. Mike plays soccer.
j. Cristina went on vacation.

18 **Interaction**

Interview your classmates until you find two students who say *yes* to each of
these questions. Report what you find to the class.

Question	Name	Name
1. Did you go to a movie last week?	Monica	Tiko
2. Can you skate?		
3. Should you study more?		
4. Do you live in an apartment?		
5. Does your brother or sister speak English?		
6. Are you a creative person?		
7. Do you often read American newspapers or magazines?		
8. Do you like rock music?		
9. Do your parents live in this country?		
10. Do you have back problems?		

Now report what you found to the class.

> Monica went to a movie last week, and so did Tiko.

19 Reading

Before You Read

1. Do you have back problems? Do you know anyone with back problems?
2. Who gets back pain? Children? Older people?
3. How can you avoid back pain?

Useful vocabulary:

1. **posture** = how you sit or stand
2. **stool**
3. **pillow**

Back pain is one of the most common health problems in the United States. It affects people of all ages and in all occupations.

If you have back pain or wish to avoid back pain, here are ten points to remember.

1. Practice good posture.

2. If you must stand for a long time, put one foot on a stool. Change from one foot to the other.

3. When you sit, keep one or both knees higher than your hips. Keep your back straight and supported.

4. Do not lie on your stomach. Do not read in bed, or use more than one pillow under your head.

5. Walk a lot; it's good for your back.

6. Ask your doctor to give you an exercise program, and follow his or her instructions.

7. Rest when you are tired.

8. Always bend your knees when you are lifting something.

9. Do not lift objects above the level of your elbows.

10. Talk to your doctor if you have any questions about back pain.

Comprehension

A. Read the following statements about how to avoid back pain. Say *True, False,* or *I don't know.*

1. You should lean forward when you sit.
2. You should bend your knees when you lift something.
3. You shouldn't do any kind of exercise.
4. You shouldn't smoke.
5. You should sleep with two or three pillows under your head.
6. You should go to bed early.

B. Now answer these questions.

1. How many of the ten suggestions to avoid back pain do you follow?
2. Can you add any suggestions to the list?

20 Writing

Write five or more points to remember for one of the following:

1. How to get a good night's sleep
2. How to stay in shape
3. How to avoid a cold

Compare your list of points with someone who wrote about the same topic.

21 Final Activity

STUDENT 1: **You had an accident, and now you are in the hospital. Your friend comes to visit. Ask him or her:**

• about the results of a game you are interested in.
• about your friends.
• about the gossip at school or in the office.
• about his or her plans for this weekend.

STUDENT 2: **You visit a friend in the hospital. He or she had an accident. Ask him or her:**

• what happened.
• how he or she is feeling.
• what the doctors say.
• when he or she can go home.

VOCABULARY: Book 2

This vocabulary list contains the productive words as well as the receptive words in Book 2. A list of vocabulary words from Book 1 is found on page 179. Productive words are those that students should know how to use. The unit number refers to when the word is first introduced productively. Receptive words are those that students need only understand. The unit number for these words is in parentheses.
(*n*) = noun; (*v*) = verb; (*adj*) = adjective; (*adv*) = adverb; (*pron*) = pronoun

A

ability (9)
above all (12)
accept (1)
accident 13
ache 13
across (7)
action (8)
activity (7)
actor (12)
add (3)
additional (1)
adjective (4)
admiration (14)
admire 12
adventure 1
adverb (11)
advice (7)
advice column (14)
affect (15)
affirmative (1)
afraid 8
again (2), 7
age (10)
agent 8
ago 8
agree (1)
aide (10)
air (9)
airline (9)
airplane 5
airport 2
album (12)
all (7)
almost (4)
alone (10)
along 6
a lot (1), 3
aloud (1)
alternative (4)
and so... 15
ankle 13

anything else (4)
apologize (14)
apology (14)
apostrophe (13)
applicant (9), 10
apply (9)
appointment 10
appropriate (12)
area (2)
arm 13
around (2)
arrival (7)
article (5)
as (1)
as a matter of fact (12)
as...as 12
as...as possible 11
at all (1)
at first (10)
at least (7), 11
at the corner of 2
at the end of 2
at times (5)
ate 13
athlete 11
attend (10)
aunt 8
auto (9)
automobile (13)
average (10)
avoid (13)
away (14)

B

back (*n*) 13
back (*adv*) (7)
backache 13
badly 11
bag 8
baggage 8
ball (11)
bank teller 9

barbecue (15)
baroque (6)
baseball player 11
based on (7)
basketball player 11
been (10)
beach 6
bean 5
beat 11
beautifully 11
became (12)
because (1), 3
bed 1
before (5)
before last 14
before yesterday 14
begin 6/began (12)
believe (5)
bell (7)
belong (14)
below (1)
bend (15)
benefit (9)
best (1)
better 14
between 2
big 12
bilingual 9
birth (12)
blank (10)
block 2
board (*v*) 8
body (13)
boot 4
border 6
bored with 9
boring (12)
boss (10)
both 14
bottom (6)
bought (4), 5
bracelet 5
break/broke 13

breathtaking (1)
bridge 2
bright 7
British (7)
brochure (6)
broke 13
bulletin (15)
bus driver (8)
bus station (2)
buy 5/bought (4), 5
by the way (3)

C

caller (10)
calm 11
came 11
came in 11
camera (5)
cannot (14)
canyon 6
careful 9
caring 9
carpenter 9
case (4)
cash (4)
castle (6)
Celsius (C) 3
certain (13)
certainly (6)
challenging (10)
change (2)
character (4)
charge (4)
chart (1)
check-in counter 8
chess 11
chess player 11
choose (6)/chose (9)
chore (7)
church 2
citizen (12)
classmate (4)

clean 7
climb (6)
close to (12)
clothes 4
cloudy 3
club (11)
coach 11
coat 4
coffee shop 2
combine (13)
come by (3)
come in (3)
come on 14
come out (3)
comedy 1
coming (7)
common (15)
commuter rail (2)
company (co.) (9)
comparative (14)
compare (12)
computer (5), 9
computer
    programmer 9
considerate 14
contain (14)
continue 6
contrast (9)
convert (3)
copper 5
corn 5
corner 2
correct (1)
cotton 5
could (4), 8
country 12
country of origin (5)
countryside (7)
course (8)
cousin 12
creative 9
crop 5
cross (13)
cue (8)
curious (10)
current (10)
currently (10)
customer (4)
cut (12)

D

dancer 11
dancing 11
dark (13)
date (14)
day 9
deal with (9)
decide (3)
deep 6
definition (11)
degree 3
delightful (6)
deliver 9
departure (7)
deputy (13)
describe (3)
description (5)
desert 6
desire (12)
destination (2)
detail (1)
devoted to (12)
diary (1)
did/didn't 1
die/died (12)
different (3)
diploma (9)
direct (10)
directions (2)
disappointed (11)
disappointment (14)
discharge (8)
discuss {12)
dissatisfaction (9)
ditch (13)
divide (3)
dominate (6)
don't worry (5)
door (7)
down (6)
downtown (7)
drama 1
dread (10)
driver (9)
during 10
dynamic (12)

E

each (1)
each other (1)
ear 13
earache 13
early 1
earring 5
east of 2
editorial (9)
education 10
egotistic (12)
eight hundred 6
elbow (15)
else (5), 9
emphasize (14)
employer (9)
end (n) 2
end (v) 6
energetic 9
enjoy (1)
enough (11)
enter (13)
equal (9)
equivalent (9)
European (7)
even 11
event (8), 11
ever (9)
everybody (4)
everyone (3)
exact (13)
exactly (5)
example (4)
exchange (1)
exciting 1
exercise (3), 15
exhibit 15
exhilarating (1)
expensive (14)
experience (6), 10
explain (4)
export (to) 5
express (7)
expression (8)
extend (15)
extension (9)
extra (14)
extremely (12)
eye 13

F

fabulous (6)
face 13
fact (5)
factory 2
Fahrenheit (F) 3
fair (10)
false (1)
famous for 6
fantastic (6)
far (2), 4
far away (1)
farmer 9
fascinating 6
fashionable (7)
fast 11
feel 10
feet 6
fell 13
female (10)
few (8)
fifteen thousand 6
fifty thousand 6
fight 9
filing (9)
fill in (3)
fill out (1)
film (12)
finally (6)
find (2), 8
find out (1)
finger 13
fire 9
fire department (2)
firefighter 9
fit 4
fitting room (4)
five hundred 6
flag (8)
flight (3), 8
flight attendant 9
floor 4
flow 6
fold (8)
folder (8)
follow (1)
following (1)
foot/feet 13
foot-high (6)

for example   (2)
for long   (7)
forecast   (3)
foreign language   9
forget   (5),   14
forget about   13
forgiving   14
formal   (11)
fortunately   (14)
found   (14)
four hundred (and)
  seventeen   6
free   (1)
free time   7
frequency   (8)
friendly   (10)
from now on   (11)
from...to   6
from...until   10
front   (2)
full   (7)
full-time   (9)
funny   1
future   (7)

G

gambling   (7)
gate   8
gave   (12)
general (*adj*)   (2)
generous   (12)
German   (10),   12
get home   1
get lost   (2)
get somewhere   (11)
get that   (2)
get to   2
gift   (4)
given   (9)
glad   (1)
glove   4
go for long walks   7
go shopping   5
go swimming   1
go to bed   1
goal   (11)
going to   7
gold   5
good at   (9)

gossip   (15)
got home   1
got to   8
graduate   (10)
great   (1),   11
greatest   (7)
greet   (1),   9
greeting   (1)
grow   5
grown   (5)
guess   (5),   9
guide   (5)
guidebook   (5)
guy   (12)
gym   (11)

H

had   (1),   10
had to   8
half   (2)
half an hour   8
hand   13
happen   (7)
hard   1
harder   14
hardly   (10)
hardworking   (12),   14
has to   9
hat   4
head   (12),   13
headache   13
health problem   (13)
hear   (1)
heard   (12)
her   12
height   (6)
here it is   8
here you are   (4),   8
high   6
high school   (7)
high-quality   (5)
hill   (6)
him   (1),   12
hip   (15)
historic building   6
horror movie   1
house   (5)
how about   1
how are you doing   (15)

how deep   6
how far   6
how long   6
how often   7
how to   9
however   (1)
humane   (1)
hundred   6
hurt   13

I

I'd   (4),   12
I'll take it   (4)
I'm afraid   8
ice skater   11
ice skating   11
identify   (4)
if   (2),   15
if so   (5)
imaginary   (6)
imagination   (10)
imagine   (2)
immediate   (9)
immediately   (13)
import (from)   5
important   (2)
improve   (12)
in common   (14)
in front of   (2)
in general   (12)
in person   (9)
in shape   (12)
include   (1)
incomplete   (13)
inconsiderate   14
incorrect   (5)
indicate   (4)
indirect   (11)
inference   (12)
infinitive   (7)
information   (1)
injure   (13)
injury   (13)
instead   4
instruction   (1)
intend   (7)
intention   (7)
interest   (12)
interesting   1

international   (9)
interview (*n*)   10
interview (*v*)   (8),   10
intonation   (14)
introduce   (1)
invitation   (15)
invite   (14)
irregular   (15)
it doesn't matter   12
it's on me   (14)
item   (5)
itinerary   (7)
its   (6)

J

jacket   4
jewelry   5
job   (8),   9
job opening   (9)
journalist   9
junior high   (10)

K

kick   11
kilometer (km)   6
kind (*adj*)   (1)
king   (12)
know   (1)
know how to   9
known   (11)

L

label   (5)
lake   2
land   (6)
lane   (13)
last (*v*)   (13)
late   (12)
lawyer   9
lazy   14
learn   (9)
leather   5
leave   (7),   8/left   8
leave from   (7)
left   2
leg   13
legal   (9)

legend   (3)
leisurely   (7)
lesson   (1)
let   (5)
let's face it   (11)
let's see   (2)
letter   (1),   9
letter carrier   9
level   (15)
lie   9
life   (10)
lift   (15)
like to   9
line   (2)
list   (1)
listen to   13
listening   (15)
local   (9)
located in   (5)
location   (2)
long   4
long time   (13)
longer   14
look at   13
look for   (4),   13
look forward to   (10)
lose/lost   11
lose control   (13)
loud   (12)
luggage   8
lunchtime   (8)

M

made   (5),   13
made in   5
made of   5
magazine   9
mail   9
main   (2)
major   (3)
mall   2
manager   (9)
manner   (9)
many   (5),   6
map   (2)
mark   (2)
match (n)   11
match (v)   (7)
material   (5)

mathematician   (12)
matter   9
maze   (6)
me   11
mean (v)   (6)
mechanical   (10)
member   (4)
mentioned   (12)
mess   7
metal   5
meter   6
middle school   (10)
midnight   (8)
mile   6
million   (12)
minor   (13)
minus   (3)
miserable   (14)
miss (n)   (8)
missing   (3)
modal   (15)
modest   (12)
modifier   (5)
modify   (5)
money   (9)
moon   (6)
more than   (4)
morning   7
most   (2)
mountain   6
mouth   13
move   15
movement   (14)
movie   1
movie star   (12)
much   13
mule   (6)
multiply   (3)
musical   (12)
musician   (12)
must be   (9),   12
my   7
myself   (5)

N

name (v)   (2)
narrow   (6)
national   (7)
nationwide   (9)

natural   (5)
near to   (2)
necessary   (13)
neck   13
necklace   5
negative   (1)
nervous   10
new   (4)
next   (1),   9
nice meeting you   (10)
nine hundred   6
ninety-nine
    thousand   6
no kidding   12
noisy   (13)
north of   2
northern   (5)
nose   13
not bad   11
not much   (1)
not so good   11
note   (4)
nothing   11
noun   (4)
nurse's aide   (10)

O

object   (4)
object pronoun   (12)
observation   (13)
occupation   (9)
of course   (4),   8
office   (2)
office building   2
often   7
oil   (5)
on a...team   11
on (your) left   2
on (your) right   2
on sale   (4)
once   (6),   7
one (pron)   4
one hundred (and)...   6
one thousand   6
oncoming   (13)
opening   (9)
opera   (13)
operator   (9)
opinion   (7)

opportunity   (7)
opposite   (6)
or   12
organizational   (9)
origin   (5)
out   (3)
out of shape   11
outdo   (1)
outdoor   (1)
outgoing   9
outstanding   (11)
over   (12)
overnight   (7)
own (adj)   (1)

P

page   (2)
pain   (13)
paint (v)   7
painting   14
pair of   4
paragraph   (1)
part   (2)
party   1
passenger   (8)
passport   8
past   (1)
past tense   (10)
patient   9
pay   (9)
percent   (10)
perfect   (4)
personal   (9)
personality trait   (14)
personnel   (9)
personnel manager   (9)
photo   (12)
photograph (v)   (1)
picture   (4)
piece   (1)
pillow   (15)
place   (1),   6
place of birth   (11)
plan   (7)
player   (11),   12
point (n)   (6)
point out   (4)
police officer   (2)
polite   (8)

politician (12)
poor 11
pop singer (12)
position (10)
positive (14)
possession (12)
possible (1), 11
posture (15)
practical (7)
practice (1), 7
prediction (7)
prefer 1
preferably (9)
preference (9)
prepare (3)
preposition (2)
prepositional
  phrase (2)
present (5)
present tense (14)
pretend (5)
pretty (adv) (2), 11
pretty good 11
prime minister (12)
prior (7)
probably (3)
problem (4), 14
procedure (8)
product (5)
profession (9)
professional (12)
program 9
pronoun (11)
proud 12
public (9)
put (6), 8
pyramid 6

Q

qualification (9)
quality (9)
quickly 11

R

race 11
rainy 3
range (6)
reading (10)

real (9)
reason (1)
reasonable 14
receipt (4)
receive (4)
recently (8)
receptionist 9
record (12)
recreational (11)
redwood (7)
reference 10
refresh (10)
refuse (1)
regular (reg.) (4)
regularly (7)
relative (1)
reorder (1)
repeat (12)
replace (4)
report (n) 9
report (v) (3)
request (8)
require (13)
resort (7)
respond (1)
response (7)
rest (15)
rest stop (8)
result (10)
résumé 10
retire (11)
return (1)
rich (12)
riding (13)
right 2
right down to (6)
ring (n) 5
ring (v) (7)
river 2
roadside (13)
rock and roll (12)
rock singer (12)
role (2)
role play (11)
roll (13)
romantic 1
route (6)
run 11
runner 11
running (4), 11

S

sad 1
salary (9)
sale ad (4)
salesperson (4)
sat (11)
saw 1
save (4)
say/said 10
scale (3)
scarf/scarves 4
scary 1
school office 13
schooling (9)
schoolwork (14)
science class 13
scientist (12)
score (11)
seat 8
seat number 8
secretarial (10)
secretary 9
section (13)
selfish 14
sent (3)
sentence (1)
serious (13)
seriously (13)
service (9)
seven hundred 6
several (2)
sew 7
shape 11
share (8), 14
shop (n) (6)
shopping 5
shorter 14
should 7
show (v) (2)
shower (3)
shrine (6)
shy (12)
sightseeing (7)
signal (8)
silk 5
silly (4)
silver 5
similar (4)
simple (1)

simply (10)
singer 11
singing 11
situation (1)
six hundred 6
six thousand 6
size 4
skate 12
skier 11
skiing 11
skill (1)
slightly (13)
slipped (13)
slowly 11
smaller (6)
snowy (3)
so (3)
so (can, is, should) 15
so (do, does, did) 15
soak up (7)
soccer 11
soccer player 11
sold (12)
solution (14)
someone (7)
something (4)
somewhere (11)
sound awful 3
sound like (1)
south of 2
southeast (5)
southern (6)
speak to 13
special (8)
spectacular (7)
speech (11)
spend (14)
standard (8)
star in (12)
state (6)
statement (1)
station 2
stay (n) (10)
step (6)
still (adv) 15
stomach 13
stomachache 13
stool (15)
stop 8
stop by (7)

stopover   (8)
storm   (3)
story   1
straight   (15)
stress   (14)
strong   (13)
study period   (7)
subtract   (3)
subway station   2
subway system   (2)
such as   (4)
sugarcane   5
suggestion   (1)
suitcase   8
sun   (3)
sunny   3
sunshine   (7)
superb   (6)
supported   (15)
suppose   (12)
survey   (10)
sweater   4
swimmer   11
swimming   1
symbol   (3)
system   (2)

T

table   (13)
take   2/took   (3)
take seriously   (14)
take turns   (1)
talk about   (3),   13
talk to   (4),   13
tap dancer   (12)
teaching   (10)
team   11
teenage   (14)
teenager   (12)
telephone   (1),   9
tell   (1),   2/told   (13)
temperature   3
temple   6
tennis   12
tennis player   11
tense   (1)
terminal   (9)
test result   15
text   (6)

than   (4)
that   4
that's right   3
that's true   (11)
the...before...   14
them   (1),   11
there are   6
there is   2
there's   2
think   (2),   7
think about   13
think so   (2)
thirty-five   (6)
those   4
thousand   6
three hundred   6
throat   13
through   6
thumb   13
thunderstorm   (3)
ticket   8
tied   11
tight   4
times   7
tired of   9
toe   13
too   4
too much   (13)
top hat   (13)
topic   (14)
tour   (7)
tourist   (2)
tournament   (12)
traffic light   2
training   (9)
transfer   (7)
travel   (8),   9
tree   (7)
truck   13
trucking   (9)
true   (1)
try   (2)
try on   4
turn   (2)
turned-on   (10)
twice   7
two hundred   6
two-thirds   (10)
two-word   (13)
type   9

U

uh   (7)
uncle   8
under   (13)
unfold   (8)
unforgiving   14
unhurt   (13)
universal   (7)
unreasonable   14
unselfish   14
until   (3)
unusual   (12)
up   (2)
upset   14
us   11
use   (4)
useful   (2)
usually   1

V

vacation   9
vegetation   (7)
verb   (1)
view   (6)
visitor   (6)
vocabulary   (2)
volleyball player   11

W

wait   (3),   8
wait for   13
walk (*n*)   7
way   (1)
we'd   (9)
we'll   (10)
we're   (10)
well   11
went   1
west of   2
western   1
wet   (5)
what a...   14
what about   1
what else   9
what happened   11
what kind of   1
what's the matter   9

what's the matter
   with...   13
wheat   5
when's   (3)
while   (13)
who's   12
whole   (6)
why don't   1
why's that   12
wide   6
wildlife park   6
will   (5)
win   11
wind   (5)
window seat   8
windy   3
wish   (9),   12
without   (9)
won   11
wonder   (7)
wonderful   (11)
wood   9
wool   5
word processing   (9)
words per minute
   (wpm)   (9)
world-famous   6
worried   15
worry   (5)
worry about   13
worse   14
would   (4)/
   wouldn't   (9)
would like to   9
wow   (3)
wrist   13
write out   (14)
write to   13
writer   (12)
wrote   (1)

Y

year   (7)
year of birth   (11)
you'll   (6)
yours   (1)

VOCABULARY: Book 1

A

a   1
ability   (5)
about   11
ache   12
across from   7
activity   (4)
actor   1
actress   1
ad   (7)
add   9
address   3
adult   (12)
advertisement   (7)
advice   (12)
after   17
afternoon   1
aged   (11)
agency   11
airplane   (5)
airport   (6)
aisle   7
algebra   16
a little   5
all   (3), 7
all over   (12)
almost never   13
a lot of   (6), 1, 5
alphabet   (2)
also   7
altitude   (13)
always   13
am   1
American   5
an   1
and   2
announcer   (8)
another   6
answer   3
any   15
anything   7
apartment   11
apple   7
appointment   5
April   3
architect   (13)

are   1
arrive   (15)
artist   1
ask for   2
aspirin   12
at   3
athletic   (5)
Atlantic   (13)
at night   8
August   3
autumn   13
avenue (ave.)   3
awful   8

B

babysit   4
back (n)   12
backache   12
bacon   (10)
bad   (13)
bag   7
baked potato   (10)
banana   7
bank   6
baseball   12
basement   (18)
basil   (9)
basketball   3
basketball court   4
bathroom   3
bay   (6)
be   1
be back   (9)
be born   (5), 14
be broke   (10)
be careful   (12)
be late   (13)
be like   6
beach   (2), 12
beans   7
beautiful   (4), 8
because   13
bedroom   3
beef   7
before   17
beige   16

best in town   (10)
better   12
beverage   (10)
bicycle (bike)   3
big   6
biology   16
birth certificate   (3)
birthday   (16), 17
black   16
blond   17
blouse   16
blue   16
board   3
boarding   (17)
boat   17
bone   (7)
boneless   (7)
book   1, 4
bookstore   6
born   1, 4
both   (14)
bottle   7
boulevard (blvd.)   3
box   7
boy   (11), 16
boy (exclamation)   10
boyfriend   2
Brazil   5
Brazilian   5
bread   7
breakfast   9
bridge   (18)
bring   (14)
brother   2
brown   16
brownies   (9)
buck   (10)
building   (13)
bun   (10)
bus   (14), 17
business   (8)
bus station   6
busy   4
but   5
butter   7
buy   7
by   17
bye   1

C

cab   17
cabbage   7
cafeteria   (5)
cake   7
call (v)   3
can/can't   5
can (n)   7
candy   6
candy store   6
canned   7
cantaloupe   (7)
capital (adj)   2
capital (n)   (13)
caption   (5)
car   3
card   (17)
carrot   (7)
cart   (7)
cartoon   (8)
cashier   1
cat   3
caution   (12)
Celsius   (13)
cent   10
center   (18)
cereal   7
channel   8
checkout   (7)
cheese   7
cheeseburger   (10)
chemistry   16
chicken   7
child/children   2
China   5
Chinese   (2), 5
choice   (7)
chopped (nuts)   (9)
church   6
cinema   (8)
citizenship   (17)
city   3
city hall   6
clarinet   5
class   5
clean   4

cleaning products   (7)
clerk   16
climate   (13)
close (v)   1
closet   3
clothes   (18)
clothing   (17)
c'mon   (4)
coast   (13)
cocoa   (9)
coffee   7
coin   18
cola   10
cold (adj)   13
cold (n)   12
cold medicine   12
cole slaw   (10)
coliseum   (6)
Colombia   5
Colombian   5
color   16
combination   10
combine   (9)
come   3
come along   6
come from   (8)
commercial   8
common   (9)
community college   6
complete   (13)
computer
programming   (7), 11
concert   8
concourse   (18)
congratulations   16
cook   1
cooking (n)   8
cool (v)   (9)
cool (adj)   13
copy   (9)
corn   7
corned beef   (10)
cost   10
cough   12
cough drops   12
country   5
couple of bucks   (10)
court   4
cousin   (5)
cuisine   (18)

cup   (9), 10
customer   16

D

dad   3
dairy product   (7)
dance   5
date   5
date filed   (3)
date issued   (3)
date of birth   14
daughter   2
day   (6), 8
day off   8
dead   15
dear (salutation)   (14)
deceased   15
December   3
deck   (18)
delicious   9
dentist   12
dessert   (18)
difficult   (13)
dime   10
dining room   3
dinner   9
direction   (18)
dish (food)   (9)
dishes   11
district   (18)
divorced   15
dizzy   12
do   1; don't   8
doctor   1
does/doesn't   8
dog   3
dollar   10
dozen   7
draw   5
dress   16
drew   (13)
drink   10
drive   5
drove   18
drug   6
drugstore   6
drums   5
dry   9
duchess   (5)

dumb   8
during   8

E

ear   12
earache   12
east   3
easy   16
eat   9
egg   7
eight   1
eighteen   1
eighteenth   5
eighth   5
eighty   2
electrician   1
eleven   1
eleventh   5
else 7
embassy   (17)
end   (16)
engineer   1
engineering   8
English   5
enter   (17)
evening   1
every   8
everyone   (8)
everything   (2), 10
everywhere   (17)
exam   5
excellent   8
excited   17
excuse me   2
extra large   16

F

Fahrenheit   (13)
fall (n)   13
family   2
famous   (5)
farewell   (1)
fast   5
fast food   (18)
father   2
favor   7
favorite   (7), 9

February   3
feel   12
feel (well)   12
feet   (13)
fever   12
fifteen   1
fifteenth   5
fifth   5
fifty   2
fill out   (17)
find   (6)
fine   1
finish   15
fire station   6
first   5
first name   3
five   1
fix   4
flew   18
flight   (13), 17
floor   (18)
floor plan   7
flour   7
flu   12
fly   (5), 17
food   7
football   5
for   9
for + (time)   9
foreign   (17)
form   3
forty   2
four   1
fourteen   1
fourteenth   5
fourth   5
France   5
free   (18)
French   5
french fries   (10)
fresh   (7), 9
Friday   3
friend   2
friendly   (5)
from   5
from (time) to (time)   8
front   (12)
frozen   9
frozen food   7
fruit   7

full name   3
fun   (11)

G

gallon (gal)   7
game   (5), 8
garage   3
garden center   (7)
garlic   (9)
gate   (17)
gave   (5)
gentlemen   (18)
geometry   16
get   10
get a (cold, flu)   12
get a gift   (16)
get going   (14)
get some rest   12
gift shop   18
gift wrapped   (16)
girl   (11), 16
girlfriend   2
give   1
glass   10
glasses   17
go   4; goes   8
go out   11
gold   (18)
good   9
good afternoon   1
good-bye   1
good evening   1
good morning   1
good night   1
grandchildren   15
granddaughter   15
grandfather   15
grandmother   15
grandparents   15
grandson   15
grape   7
graph   (11)
gray   16
greased (pan)   (9)
great   1
green   16
greeting   (1)
group   3
guitar   5

H

hair   17
half gallon   7
ham   (10)
hamburger   (10)
happy   (13), 17
harbor   (18)
hard   (13), 16
has   8
has to   15
hate   13
have   8
have to   4
Hawaii   (13)
he   1
he's   1
head   12
headache   12
head of lettuce   9
health professional
   (12)
heaven   (18)
height   (17)
helicopter   (5)
hello   1
help   (5), 11
her   2
here   6
here's   6
here comes   (2)
hey   5
hi   1
his   2
history   16
home   3
homemaker   1
homework   (11)
hon   (7)
honey   12
Hong Kong   (13)
hope (v)   12
hope so   16
horizon   (18)
horse   (5)
hospital   3
hot   13
hot chocolate   (10)
hot dog   7
hotel   6

hour   (8), 9
house   (4)
housework   11
how   1
how's   1
how about   7
how are you   1
how many   9
how much   9
how much (cost)   10
how old   11
how's everything   1
how's it going   (7)
hundred   2
hungry   10
hurt   12
husband   2

I

I   1
I'll   3
I'm   1
ice cream   7
iced (coffee/tea)   (10)
ice skate   13
idea   4
identification   (17)
identifying   2
if   2
if not   (15)
immigration official
   (14)
in   3
in fact   (14)
including   (18)
incredible   (18)
information   (3)
ingredients   (9)
instrument   (5)
interesting   8
interior   (13)
international   (17)
interviewer   (13)
into   9
introduce   (13)
is   1
isn't   1
it   1
it's   1

it sure does   (8)
Italian   5
Italy   5
item   (7)

J

jacket   (18)
January   3
Japan   5
Japanese   5
jeans   16
job   (10)
juice   7
July   3
jumbo   (10)
June   3
just   3

K

ketchup   7
key ring   18
kids   2
kilometer   (13)
kind (n)   (9)
kitchen   3
Korea   5
Korean   5

L

ladies and gentlemen
   (9)
language   5
large   (7), 9
largest   (13)
last month   13
last name   3
last night   13
last week   13
last year   13
late   (8)
later   1
laundry   11
leave for   (14)
lemon   12
lemonade   (10)
length   (17)
let's   4

letter   (5)
lettuce   7
librarian   (8)
library   6
lie down   12
like + *(n)*   8
like to + *(v)*   10, 13
liquid   12
listed   (7)
listen to   1
little   16
live *(v)*   8
living room   3
loaf/loaves   7
located   (13)
location   (6)
long   17
look + *(adj)*   9
look at   1
look for   16
look like   (6)
look up   (5)
love   13
lunch   9

M

ma'am   7
major (13)
make   8
man/men   16
manage   (11)
manager   (7)
many   (9)
map   (6)
March   3
margarine   7
marina   6
married   2
marvelous   8
master *(adj)*   (13)
math   (10)
May   3
may I help you   (7), 16
maybe   (10), 12
mayonnaise   (7)
me   7
me too   10
meal   (18)
mean   6

measurement   (9)
meat   7
mechanic   1
medium   10
meet   1
melon   (7)
melted   (9)
menu   (10)
met   14
meter   (13)
Mexican   5
Mexico   5
middle initial   3
middle name   3
midnight   (18)
midtown   (18)
mile   (13)
milk   7
minute   3
mix   (9)
model   18
modern   (13)
Mom   (3)
Monday   3
month   (3), 15
more   (18)
morning   1
most   (11)
mother   2
move   3
movies   4
Mr.   1
Mrs.   1
Ms.   1
mug   18
museum   6
mushroom   9
music   4
mustard   (7)
my   1
my place   (4)

N

name   1
nasal spray   12
nation   (18)
nationality   5
navy   (5)
near   6

need   7
nervous   17
never   13
news   8
newspaper   4
newsstand   (17)
next month   15
next summer   15
next to   (5), 7
next week   15
next year   15
nice   1
nice to meet you   1
nickel   10
nickname   3
night   1
nine   1
nineteen   1
nineteenth   5
ninety   2
ninth   5
no   1
noon   1
north   3
nose   12
not   3
not bad   16
not exactly   (5)
not too good   12
note   (4)
nothing much   15
November   3
now   10
number   3
nurse   1
nursing a baby   (12)
nuts   (9)

O

o'clock   4
oatmeal   7
observation deck   (18)
October   3
of   7
offer   (18)
office   3
oh   2
oh no   5
oil   7

OK   1
old   (6), 9
older   (12)
on   6
on sale   (7)
one   1
one *(pronoun)*   17
onion   7
only   10
open   1
optional   (9)
or   11
orange *(n)*   7, *(adj)*
   16
order   10
oregano   (9)
originally   5
other   (5), 12
ounce (oz)   7
our   2
out loud   3
outside   (11)
over there   7

P

package   7
pain   (12)
pain relief   (12)
paint   4
painting *(n)*   (18)
pair   16
pan   9
pants   16
paper   1
paper goods   (7)
parents   2
park *(n)*   4
parking lot   3
partner   3
part-time   (10)
pass (an exam)   16
passenger   (13)
passport   (17)
pastrami   (10)
pear   7
peas   7
pen   6
penny   10
people   2

pepper   7
pepperoni   10
permit   (17)
person   2
pharmacist   (12)
phone   3
physician   (12)
physics   16
piano   5
pick up   12
pickle   (10)
picture   (1)
piece of paper   1
pilot   (5)
pinch of   (9)
pink   16
pint   7
pizza   10
place   (4)
plain   10
plan   (13)
plane   (5), 17
plastic   18
plate (dish)   (10)
play (v)   4
please   3
plenty of   12
point   3
police officer   1
police station   6
pool   4
Portuguese   5
possibility   (18)
postcard   18
poster   18
post office   6
potato   7
potato chips   7
pound (lb)   7
pour   9
powder   (9)
pregnant   (12)
pretty (adj)   (6)
price   10
prince   (5)
print   (3)
problem   (4)
program   8
programming   (7)
pronounce   6

purchase   (18)
pure (beef)   (10)
purple   16
put   9
put away   1

Q

quart (qt)   7
quarter   10
queen   (5)
question   3

R

racquet   (4)
rain (v)   (13)
rarely   13
read   3
ready   (13)
really + (adj)   (8)
recipe   8
red   16
regards to   (14)
registration card   (3)
relax   4
required   (18)
rest   12
restaurant   1
restaurant cashier   1
rice   7
ride   5
right   3
right away   12
right here   6
right now   (7)
river   (18)
road (rd.)   3
rock (music)   (8)
rock concert   12
roller skate   5
room   3
run   5
Russian   5

S

sad   17
salad   9
salt   7
same   (11)

sandals   16
sandwich   (10)
Saturday   3
sausage   7
sauce   8
saw (v)   14
say   1
schedule   (8)
school   3
season (n)   13
season (v)   9
second   5
see   1
see you then   12
seek   (12)
sentence   3
September   3
set   18
seven   1
seventeen   1
seventeenth   5
seventh   5
seventy   2
share   11
she   1
she's   1
shirt   16
shoes   16
shop   (18)
shopper   (7)
shopping   (18)
shopping list   (9)
short   3
shorts   16
should   12
sick   14
side order   (10)
sing   5
single   15
sir   10
sirloin   (7)
sister   2
sit   3
sit down   3
site   (13)
six   1
sixteen   1
sixteenth   5
sixth   5
sixty   2

size   16
skate   13
ski   5
skinny   17
skirt   16
skyscraper   (18)
slacks   16
sleep   4
slice (v)   9
slice (n)   10
sliced (eggs)   (10)
slicing (tomatoes)   (7)
small   6
smart   (8)
smell   9
snack bar   (18)
snack foods   (7)
sneakers   16
snow   (3)
so + (adj)   (15)
soccer   5
socks   16
soda   10
soft drinks   7
some   7
something   10
sometimes   13
son   2
soon   12
sore throat   12
sorry   4
sound good   10
soup   7
south   3
South America   13
souvenir   18
Soviet Union   5
spaghetti   7
Spanish   5
speak   5
speaking   (7)
split   (10)
sponsor   (8)
sports   8
sports events   (6)
spring   13
square (adj)   (9)
stadium   (6)
stand up   3
state   (3)

Statue of Liberty   18
stay   (15)
stay at   18
stay home   15
steak   (7)
still *(adv)*   (14)
stomach   12
stomachache   12
stop *(v)*   (7)
stop *(n)*   (17)
store   6
street (st.)   3
student   1
study   4
study for   (4)
stuffy   12
subway   (18)
sugar   7
suggest   (4)
suit   16
summer   (7), 13
Sunday   3
super discount   (7)
supermarket   6
sure   (5), 7
swim   5
swiss cheese   (10)

T

T-shirt   16
tablespoon   9
tablet   (12)
take   16
take care   1
take care of   8
take out   1
talented   (5)
talk   (6)
tall   17
taste   9
taxi   17
tea   7
teach   8
teacher   (3), 8
team   (8)
teaspoon   (9)
technical institute
   (7), 8
telephone company   3

telephone number   3
telephone operator   2
temperature   (13)
ten   1
tennis   (4)
tenth   5
terrible   12
terrific   8
test   (7)
thanks   1
thank you   1
that   2
that's   2
that's fine   7
the   2
theater   6
their   2
then   12
there   3
these   2
they   2
they're   2
thing   (5)
third   5
thirsty   10
thirteen   1
thirteenth   5
thirtieth   5
thirty   2
thirty-first   5
this   1
this week   15
three   1
throat   12
through   8
Thursday   3
ticket   12
tie   16
time   4
tired   (10), 12
to   1
toasted   (10)
today   1
told   (12)
tomato   7
tomato paste   (9)
tomorrow   1
tonight   1
too   (5), 16
too bad   4

took   18
tooth   12
toothache   12
top   (18)
town   (10)
trade   (18)
train   17
train station   6
travel   (7), 11
travel agent   1
trip   17
Tuesday   3
tuna   (10)
turkey   (7)
turn on   (8)
TV   4
TV guide   (8)
twelfth   5
twelve   1
twentieth   5
twenty   1
twenty-eight   2
twenty-eighth   5
twenty-fifth   5
twenty-first   5
twenty-five   2
twenty-four   2
twenty-fourth   5
twenty-nine   2
twenty-ninth   5
twenty-one   2
twenty-second   5
twenty-seven   2
twenty-seventh   5
twenty-six   2
twenty-sixth   5
twenty-third   5
twenty-three   2
twenty-two   2
two   1
typical   (10), 11

U

uh   5
understand   6
United States   5
university   (6)
us   4
use   9

usually   (6), 13

V

vacation   17
vanilla   (9)
varies   (13)
vegetable   7
very   5
Vietnam   5
Vietnamese   5
view   (18)
village   (18)
violin   5
visa   (17)
visit   (5)
voice   (3)
volleyball   5

W

wait a minute   (8)
waiter   10
waitress   10
walk   17
want + *(n)*   (6), 10
warm   13
warning   (12)
was/were   13
wash   4
watch *(v)*   4
watch *(n)*   4
water   10
watermelon   (7)
way   16
we   2
wear   16
weather   13
Wednesday   3
week   11
weekend   11
weight   (17)
welcome to   (1)
well . . .   1
well   12
went   14
were   13
we're   2
west   3
what   1